THE YOGA

OF THE CHRIST

M. MacDONALD-BAYNE

M.C., PH.D., D.D.

(Principal: College of Universal Science)

Author of: *The Higher Power You Can Use, I am the Life, Heal Yourself, Spiritual and Mental Healing, What is Mine is Thine (Parts I and II), How to Relax and Revitalise Yourself, Divine Healing of Mind and Body (The Master Speaks Again), Your Life Renewed Every Day (The Greatest Tonic in the World)*

Published by Audio Enlightenment Press.Com

Giving Voice to the Wisdom of the Ages

Printed in the United States of America

First Printing, 2014

1 2 3 4 5 6 7 8 9 10

ISBN 978-1-941489-14-7

www.AudioEnlightenmentPress.Com

A GNOSTIC AUDIO SELECTION

First AudioEnlightenmentPress.Com Printing
April 2014

EDITOR'S FOREWORD

Dr. Murdo MacDonald-Bayne was born in Scotland in 1887. During his lifetime he traveled throughout the world healing thousands of people of all kinds of diseases, and teaching the Truth of the Law of Being to many thousands more. Murdo MacDonald-Bayne was fondly referred to as Dr.Mac by his students, who often spoke of seeing him overshadowed by a higher being during his lectures. It is said that he journeyed several times into India and Tibet where he spent long periods (recounted in *Beyond the Himalayas* and its sequel, *The Yoga of the Christ*) in the company of true Masters of the Tibetan Himalayas.

He often spoke about his books and teachings being undiscovered for a period of time and then entering a new era of resurgence. I believe now is the time for people to discover, or rediscover, the works of this great man.

This edition is based on the original manuscripts and we have kept the original spellings of words (i.e. criticise instead of criticize, organisations instead of organizations) to keep the integrity of the original manuscript. It is our purpose to maintain and present lost spiritual classics, not to edit them to meet our needs.

This is also a Gnostic Audio Selection, which means that in addition to an incredible read, you have access to the streaming audio book version, for those days when you just want to kick back and enjoy a great audio book. Information for accessing the streaming audio is in the resource section at the back of the book.

We are republishing *The Yoga of the Christ* (as well as *Beyond the Himalayas*) by Dr.Bayne, and more titles when they become available. If you are a student of spirituality and metaphysics you owe it to yourself to read the works of this incredible healer and teacher.

Barry J. Peterson

TABLE OF CONTENTS

To the Reader of this book:

My wish for you is:

May God bless and keep you safe and well,

now and always.

Yours very sincerely,

M. MACDONALD-BAYNE

FOREWORD

The Christ Yoga is Christ Consciousness and is beyond all other Yoga. The Christ Yoga is Freedom, and without freedom there is no Christ Consciousness---there is merely the self which is burdened with system, with knowledge, with technique.

It will be seen, as we progress, that desire and search have their opposites, their resistance. All desires and searching are but an extension of the self, which is not the Real. The Christ Yoga is to understand all that is hiding the Real---the Christ. Therefore it is entirely different from all other types of Yoga, which are merely systems which demand a searching in which there is no finding. Thus "becoming" is an illusion. Reality is *NOW*.

Now it is important to bear in mind that there is difficulty in understanding that which is new---ever-renewing. We can understand what the mind is made up of, but it is what the mind is made up of that causes all the resistance to the new, to the Real.

So in reading this book it is essential to read it aloud and listen as if you were listening to someone else without resistance, without prejudice, and only in this way can the mind know itself with all its opposites, its beliefs, and fabrications.

What I am going to say now is very important for you who are embarking on the road to Freedom---the Christ Yoga.

Most people listen casually; they only hear what they want to hear---they shut themselves off from what is penetrating or disturbing their conditioning, their beliefs, their opinions. They listen only to the things that are pleasureable, satisfying their own conditioning.

But there can be no real understanding if we listen only to those things that soothe us, that gratify or confirm our beliefs, our ideas.

It is an art to listen to everything without prejudice, with-out building up defences to protect our ignorance, our confirmed beliefs, our original knowledge, our particular idiosyncrasies and our own points of view, and listen to find out the truth of the matter.

For it is only the truth that fundamentally frees us---not conclusions or speculations, but the perception of what is not true. What the mind is made up of is not Truth; the Truth is beyond mind, so the mind must cease to formulate before Truth is revealed.

The truth of the matter can never be revealed to a mind that is narrow, bigoted, conditioned with beliefs and knowledge that is binding and blinding.

The Christ Yoga is impossible to anyone who approaches it with a mind that is cluttered with private conclusions, prejudices and experiences. The Christ Yoga is the Love, the Wisdom of God---the Christ free and active, not merely an idea of It, which is a hindrance to Its Creativeness. An idea is but the projection of the self with all its conditioning surrounding it.

So, when listening, do not merely listen to the word but to the inward content of it, and thus you will discover the truth of the matter for yourself. When the mind is freed from its own formulations, only then is Truth uncovered.

When you are caught up in your daily struggles, in your fears, in your business worries, family quarrels, social enmities and frustrations, these may be too much for you. So you pursue the so-called Truth as a means of relief, but this form of escape can never solve any problem; it only dulls the mind while the confusion remains. As long as the mind is trying to escape through stimulations and so-called inspiration, through prayer or repeating mantrims, it is incapable of understanding its own process which is essential to freedom.

Self-knowledge is the only way. All forms of escape take you away from the fundamental principle underlying the Christ Yoga.

So, in listening, it is not the accumulation of ideas that will set you free, nor mere conclusions, theories or speculations, for these are a hindrance to Creativeness of the Truth. Only by understanding the self with all its fabrications can it be realised that this self- knowledge is the doorway to Truth, the gateway to the christ Yoga.

CHAPTER I

This book, *The Yoga of the Christ,* is a continuation of and a sequel to my last book *Beyond the Himalayas,* and it describes the never-to-be forgotten sojourn with my friend, the journey to Zamsar and back to so-called civilisation as we know it, to fulfill the task allotted to me.

The glorious revealing of the Christ Yoga is beyond price, and it is the foundation of the coming age when Love and Wisdom will prevail. What we know now as a civilisation will be as ashes like similar civilisations of the past.

After we left the Hermit of Ling-Shi-La we both agreed that it would be better to reach the quiet of my friend's sanctuary at Zamsar before we commenced our real work of the Yoga of the Christ, so we left it at that. In the mean-time we would enjoy each other's companionship on the way, and every step of the way would be a revealing process to me.

After crossing the Tsang Po (the great Brahmaputra) we took shelter in a cave beside the river for the night. There we found some dry wood and it lit a roaring fire on which we cooked some food we had taken with us. We kept the fire going well into the night and talked about the Hermit and his life. I fell asleep and did not wake until the sun rose. It was cold but I felt refreshed and went down to the river to have a wash. When I returned, breakfast was ready and we ate, and then made our way towards the trade route to Lhasa, retreading our steps as far as a place called Dikyiling. From here we took the path to the left running along a river called the Rang Chu, and then we linked up with the trade route along the side of the great lake called Yamdrok Tso, sometimes called Lake Palti or the Turquoise Lake (because of its colour).

It took us three days to reach this point, the going being extremely rough, just a mere narrow two-foot path, but eventually we reached the trade route which meant comparatively easy going. When we reached a small town called Pede Dzong my friend called on the headman whom he knew well and he supplied us with two ponies. I was glad to have that faithful Tibetan pony all the way to Zamsar and back. My mount was a stallion, jet black, not a spot of white anywhere, and very sure-footed. I named him Black Prince. At first he was a little fresh, but he settled down as we got to know each other. One gift I always had was that of getting on well with horses, for I had been brought up with them in my early life.

I can remember, when I was quite young, that we had a very wild black stallion called Black Prince. None of the others dared go near him, yet I could enter his loose box and feed him with linseed cake which he chewed with relish. One day my parents saw me feeding him and they were extremely distressed, indeed they forbade me to do such a thing again. Yet I loved that horse and at no time did he try to kick or bite me. From then onwards I was supposed to have what was known as the horseman's word. What that meant I did not know, and it was considered to be a secret. Yet I am convinced that there is no such thing as a horseman's word, only a response to love that one has for animals. My Tibetan pony reminded me of Black Prince, and hence his name.

My friend and I spoke about things in general on our way, for we had already decided not to pursue our real work till we reached Zamsar.

For miles we wandered on, taking in what we saw. My thoughts often strayed to the sanctuary of the Hermit of Ling-Shi-La and what had been revealed to me there. To me the Hermit was a real memory, and much of what he had said was unfolding in my mind as we went on our way. My thoughts and those of my friend were often very much the same; many times we would speak of the same things.

Chapter I

On the third day we reached the Turquoise Lake. "So this is Yamdrok Tso," I said. It could well be a loch in the Highlands of Scotland where I was born, with an island not far from the shore and, beyond, the mountains covered with snow. The water was of a greenish blue which gave it the name of Turquoise Lake. No wind was blowing and the surface was calm. I got off my pony and went down to the water's edge. From there I could see plenty of fish swimming around, hundreds of them. My angler's eye fastened on a few and I wished I had a rod and line just then.

"What an angler's paradise!" I said to my friend.

"Yes," he replied, "I could see the glint in your eye but we have no time for fishing now."

Here we were, 14,000 feet above sea level, and it was fresh even though the sun was shining. The lakeside was covered with wild flowers, making a profusion of colour.

"What a sanctuary," I said, for there were hundreds of wild duck and geese on the lake. I picked up a stone and threw it into the water near them and off they flew, quacking over to the island about half a mile away.I felt joyful---the scene was so lovely, with life all around us, and the roughest part of the journey over. All day we rode along the lakeside, and we passed several trains of yak and donkeys carrying loads both ways. In one train I counted more than 500 yaks and in another train I counted 150 donkeys.

The village of Pede Dzong juts out into the lake, and right on the farthest protruding part stands an old fort. It reminded me of Glen Urquhart Castle jutting out into Loch Ness of Inverness-shire in Scotland. Around the ruins were patches of wild flowers; blue and violet delphiniums were there in profusion, with other wild flowers such as gentian, etc.

We made two halts on the way, cooked our food and slept in our sleeping bags. The only things that troubled me were the mosquitoes.

We travelled around the lake till we came again to the Tsang Po, after crossing the Nyapso La. From this pass, 16,000 feet up, we could look down the valley of the Tsang Po, and as far as the eye could reach I could see the valley was covered with green, red and brown patches of cultivation through which the great Tsang Po flows.

Here and there the high ground on each side of the river was dotted with houses with red roofs, and on the far side was a great range of mountains covered with snow. I gazed upon it for some time and then I heard my friend's voice calling: "Where are you?" for he had gone ahead.

I replied: "Coming", and I could hear my voice echoing down the valley. It was a sheer sensation, and I recall it as I write.

Down we went zigzagging for nearly 5,000 feet and then we came upon this very fertile valley. The wild flowers were in profusion over two feet high. Never had I seen such an array of colour. There were blue and violet delphiniums, primulas and gentians, wild rhubarb and Chinese poppies and may other wild flowers.

Where the track reaches the Tsang Po the river is over a quarter of a mile wide and it flows very rapidly. I threw a piece of wood into the surging mass of water, and the wood sped away at the rate of about thirty miles an hour.

The Tsang Po was in spate, the snows from the great Himalayas were melting, and recently there had been heavy rains lasting some days. We rested at a place called Changda Dzong. My friend was known all along the trade route, and we were made welcome in well. Next day we proceeded down the side of the river to Chaksam. Here we crossed without incident on a ferry made from trees with spars tied across them, holding them together. Although the river was at this time considered dangerous, we reached the other side safely, more than half a mile down from our starting point.

Here the river widens several miles and winds its way through the sand wastes as far as the eye could see.

The track now on the other side of the river zigzagged up and down, sometimes high above the river and then down again by the riverside, till we reached the Kyi Chu, a river almost as wide as the Tsang Po. (Kyi Chu means river of happiness.) Here these two great rivers meet, the Kyi Chu coming down from Lhasa and the Tsang Po running into it. At the meeting of these two snow rivers there was great turbulence, whirlpools hundreds of feet wide whirling and surging, aggravated by the swollen waters. No living thing could last in this torrent of rushing snow-water for more than a minute; even a boat would be swamped and sucked down in the whirling mass of water which was once ice and snow.

We watched this terrific struggle going on as the waters met.

I said: "I don't think there is anywhere in the world a sight like this."

"No," my friend assented, "this is one of the great sights of the world, but few from the outside world have ever seen it."

Both rivers were now one and turned at right angles. It was still the great Brahmaputra, and Kyi Chu swallowed up in it, now one, making its way to the sea through the richest fertile area in Tibet. We could see away in the distance both sides of the river richly cultivated. Throughout this area there are a number of ferries. The first is at a place called Dorjetra, another is farther down at a place called Chitishio Dzong, another is at a place called Gerba, and yet another is at Timen, all being in a stretch of about forty to fifty miles, an area never yet visited by any Westerners.

We were still clad in the robes of the Lama and had all the privileges that are afforded them. My friend did the talking, I answering in Tibetan when asked a question; but never allowing myself to be caught up in a flowing conversation. On the way we met several Lamas who knew my friend personally as a great sage, and this put him always in the foreground.

Next day we reached Drepung Monastery, the largest monastery in the world. My friend was well acquainted with the Abbots there and we were made very welcome. My friend told them of my work and why I was in Tibet, and this created great interest among the Abbots. I was introduced to a Lama called Mundu (that was how his name was pronounced). He was educated in India and went to England to study mining engineering. He was a delightful fellow. He spoke excellent English and we had many animated talks together.

I was amazed at the size of Drepung Monastery. It is a big town, self-contained, with over 9,000 Lamas. The main hall accommodated over 6,000 Lamas at one time. The prayer wheels were the largest I have seen in Tibet; they were about ten feet in diameter and moved on cog wheels. A handle turned a large wheel which in turn turned others which turned the great wheel with ease. When one revolution of the prayer wheel was made, a gong rang which could be heard all over the entrance hall in which it stood; this was a sign that your sins were forgiven.

The ritual and all the paraphernalia were much the same as in other monasteries, like those I mentioned in my book *Beyond the Himalayas.*

I had been given comfortable quarters and good food. We stayed in Drepung only one day and one night, as we wanted to proceed to my friend's sanctuary at Zamsar as quickly as we could.

We decided not to waste our time with officials, so we agreed after visiting the Potala at Lhasa to go on. The Abbots were astonished at our decision. Officialdom to them was of great consequence, but to us it was merely waste of time.

As we reached the gateway leading into Lhasa we came upon a swarm of beggars sitting by the roadside, with their tongues protruding as a sign of thanks for what they expected to receive.

These beggars are professional and would not deign to do any other work. They are led by the bandits I told you about in my book *Beyond the Himalayas*. They also assume that banditry and begging are a gentleman's occupations.

From the outskirts of Lhasa the Potala looked majestic with its golden roofs shining in the sun. It stands upon that great rock upon which it was built many centuries ago, seventeen stories high, long before America was ever heard of. Yes, the Potala is perhaps the largest single building in the whole world.

We went to the Potala with written permission. The Regent was then in charge. The Dalai Lama was in Darjeeling in India at that time, having had to flee for his life. I saw most of the outstanding things including the Garden of Mystics, the Dalai Lama's tomb, etc., his throne and many other important things which make up their religion in which I was much interested; knowing what religion is, I knew that it was all made to impress.

We think that by giving a coin to a beggar we have solved the problem. We call it charity, so we feel important, we feel noble. But is it noble? Are we not all responsible for the society that permits of this tragedy in human wastage?

We see the aged, the blind, the crippled, the diseased, we see the loathsome state of affairs outside these majestic edifices built of stone, cluttered inside with riches. Yet the living are allowed to rot and die in their appalling misery. Yes, we stand branded, yet unashamed of our own miserable handiwork, in which organised religion fails to raise her head because she belongs to the society that is responsible for this state of affairs.

Yes, Lhasa is a city of beggars, filth and intrigue. There is no idea of sanitation, men and women squat down on the street like dogs. It is only the cold climate that keeps an epidemic from spreading. Dead dogs lie on the roadway, others are so emaciated that they can hardly walk, with sores all over. I felt that if I had a gun I would shoot the poor miserable beasts to free them from their misery. The dead ones are eaten by the living, for that is all the food they can find. Litters of pups are born from an emaciated bitch that can hardly crawl herself. It is a miserable sight to witness in the centre of one of the great religious places in the world. The disregard for life of all kinds, even human life, is beyond description.

Tibetans will spend any amount of time and money on their "dead" religion but have little or no interest in the living things around them; even the most primitive hygiene is sadly lacking. We see magnificent buildings, temples with golden roofs, etc., built over the dead bodies of past Dalai Lamas, yet ordinary kindness to the very least is lacking. Where is there dogma with no love or life in them.

Most of the shops, which are really stalls, are run by women. In fact they are considered better business people than the men. We got to the Post Office where we found a Lama who spoke English. He was educated in India. I posted a letter to a great friend of mine, Dan Wanberg (who has now passed from this earth life) in Johannesburg; his wife Teddy still has that letter, which she regards as one of her most cherished possessions.

Chapter I

The name Lhasa means "the place of the Gods". We visited the holiest shrine in the world, Jo-Kang. It has a golden roof which shines in the sun. This shrine was built in A.D.650 to enshrine the image of the Buddha brought by the wives of the great King Song-tsen- Gampo.

In 1925 a plague of smallpox broke out in Lhasa in which about 8,000 people died; their bodies were put into heaps and burnt outside the city, and the stench, I was told, was too terrible.

As we passed the Temple of Jo Kang we saw beggars and pilgrims alike prostrating themselves in the filth before the temple, uttering prayers all the time; they crawled along on their bellies because it would be sacrilege to walk. What has the mind of man come to when he worships a building built with hands? He grovels in the dirt debasing his very soul---the real temple of the living God. I was so disgusted by what I saw that for me the very presence of the great Potala lost all significance.

We entered the temple where there was a large figure of the Buddha covered with diamonds and precious stones, probably the most precious image in the world. Around this image were gold butter-lamps which have been kept burning without a stop for hundreds of years. We passed other shrines on the way, but to describe these would fill a book by itself.

One shrine I must mention is that of Palden Lhamo. This Buddha is equal to the Hindu God Kali, wife of Shiva. There were two images, of which showed her as a frightful monster clad in the skins of her human victims and eating the brains of others from a human skull; around her were the emblems of disease and death, hideous masks, and all the hideous contraptions for killing people. Her face was too horrible to look upon. This was what the poor deluded people had to look upon! If this is religion then the sooner we get rid of it the better, and perhaps now the Communists have occupied this so-called holy city the sooner will this so- called religion, which lives on intrigue be relegated to the scrap heap where most of its poor deceived adherents are thrown without mercy, without care or love. What I saw in the Potala I will describe in more detail in the next chapter.

Agricultural methods in Tibet today are exactly as they were a thousand years ago. The surface of the earth is still scratched with primitive ploughs, but without the winter frosts to break up the soil this ploughing would be useless.

The sound of the deep-toned cowbells which hang around the necks of the yak or dzo pulling the plough adds to the fascinating picture, which though primitive has its charm. The women, barefooted, with their skirts tucked well above the knee, walk behind the plough scattering the seeds which are immediately covered with earth by a primitive harrow made from a log of wood with hard spikes of wood pushed through holes burnt for that purpose.

As soon as the seedlings appear, the Ngak-Pa or miracle worker comes along with a large number of mud balls; and he lays a spell upon the earth, goes to the top of the nearest hill and offers prayers to the various spirits for the protection of the crop from hailstones, hailstorms being very prevalent in Tibet.

When the clouds appear on the horizon he extends the fourth finger of his right hand and blows blasts on a human thighbone and commands the storm to retire. If the storm does not obey and hail stones fall, he works himself up into a frenzy and repeats mantrims over his beads and hurls a handful of these enchanted mud balls at the storm.

If the hail passes without damaging the crop he becomes the centre of admiration and reverence from the cultivators, but should they lose their crops he not only forfeits his fee but also has to pay a fine imposed by the government. This is idiotic superstition at its best.

At harvest time all the village turns out to bring in the crops which are cut and threshed at the same time and place. A suitable piece of ground is prepared and the oxen are brought in to tread out the corn or whatever it is, and eat their fill while doing so.

The threshing is now completed with flails which consist of two pieces of wood joined together with a yak skin hinge; then the chaff is separated from the corn and packed away for cattle feed during the winter.

When the harvest is over there is great rejoicing; the people dance, drink beer to their hearts' content, many being unable to stand up. The "occasion" ends with singing and dancing.

CHAPTER II

I have now gazed upon four of the greatest religious buildings in the world: St. Paul's London, St. Peters Rome, the Holy Mosque at Khadimain on the River Tigris fourteen miles above Bhagdad, and now the Potala at Lhasa, unique and the most difficult to reach in all the world--- and all this in one lifetime. Perhaps not more than a handful of people out of the whole world have done the same.

The Potala as a religious centre represents one-fifth of the total population of the whole world. All those who follow the Buddhist religion look to the Potala at Lhasa, the seat of the great Dalai Lama, the spiritual head of all Buddhism.

The Potala is built upon a great rock in the middle of the Lhasa plains, through which the Kyi Chu flows. This majestic edifice, the Potala, stands over 400 feet high and measures nearly 1,000 feet long, and including all the out-buildings it covers an area of nearly 1 1/2 square miles, surrounded by snowcapped mountains. This towering white-washed monument of seventeen stories high was built in the sixteenth century before our western skyscrapers were even thought of. The building workmanship is perhaps the best in the world, having been built to stand through the ages. Its golden roof will still be glittering in the sun when other skyscrapers have crumbled to mere rubble. It is undoubtedly the inspired skill of some master builder, carried down through the ages.

The Potala stands out above everything for miles around. As we looked upon it in the moonlight its great whitewashed face stood out as if reflecting an eerie unseen light with dazzling brilliance. It has a magic quality; its mystery grips you as you gaze upon it.

The sky, a blue canopy overhead in which sparkled millions of twinkling stars, and the light of the full moon gave it an ethereal quality, as if we were transplanted to another world. In the distance we could hear the deep sonorous voices of the Lamas repeating the familiar formula *Om Mani Padme Hum,* and with this the deep tones of the great gongs and the sounding of the chonghas intermingling with the tinkling of hundreds of tiny bells held a fascination for me. Although I had heard all this before, yet it had this night a deeper feeling of wonderment. Yes, it was the most fascinating and magical sight and sound that could ever fall on the eyes and ears.

"Truly, there is nothing like this in the world," I said to my friend. He was deep in thought and my voice must have awakened him out of his reverie, for he looked at me in astonishment as he replied: "What did you say?"

I found I could not repeat the words, so I said: "It is truly wonderful," and he smiled as if a memory of long ago were passing through his mind.

Although the Potala is of purely Tibetan architecture, yet it reminded me of Arabia and Egypt. Not only did its colossal size take my breath away but also its colour and beauty of structure fascinated me.

It fitted into its surroundings so naturally, giving the impression that it could not have been built by man, but had in some way been just placed there by some unseen hands. The trees, the mountains capped with snow, the lake nearby, the golden pavilion shining in the moonlight, the glittering stars, the chanting sound of the Lamas' voices, the deep boom of the great gongs and sounding of the chonghas and the tinkling of hundreds of little bells, all mingling together, raised in me an indelible never-to-be-forgotten memory that seems to have lived through eternity.

My friend was well acquainted with many of the officials and he got permission for us to tour parts of the Potala the next day. I saw so much in such a short time that it is only possible to describe the highlights.

What I remember in particular was the Dalai Lama's beautiful suite of rooms. Masses of golden images and golden facings and monograms, embossed in gold, adorned the walls.

There was the throne room with its golden canopy and beautiful rich silk golden woven brocades, with deep purple and gold colouring, all blended into exquisite designs by master craftsmen.

In the Dalai Lama's tomb were hundreds of gold and silver cups and bowls, gold and silver images, gold facing on the walls, and exquisite filigree in gold and silver mounting the cases in which images studded with jewels were kept. I could not help thinking what a waste of time and money it was to house a dead decaying body. The whole thing took my breath away; I had never seen, and I suppose never will see again, such wealth locked away doing nothing for anyone.

The outside canopy of the Dalai Lama's tomb is covered with gold plate. I am sure I must have gazed upon many millions of pounds worth of gold in this building alone.

As our time was limited, and as there was more important work to do than to gaze upon all this wealth, we departed the following morning on our journey to Zamsar.

We reached the Tragtse Monastery that evening. This monastery is perched high on the mountainside. When we came within sight of it I said to my friend: "It seems an impossible task to build such a colossal building so high upon the rock face. How did the get those massive timbers and great boulders into position?" For the task seemed to me to be one beyond human endeavour.

My friend replied: "That building you see is over 600 years old and is as solid today as the day it was built. It will last another 600 years and then be as it is today."

Awaiting me was a most pleasant surprise. I saw Geshi Rimpoche coming down the steps to meet us! Apparently my friend knew, but did not "let on" to me. My heart leapt for joy when I saw his venerable face covered with a deep knowing smile as much as to say, "So you see I am here before you after all."

The joy of seeing him again dispelled the tiredness I had felt, for we had made our fifteen miles that day. Now I knew why my friend was always saying that we must make haste.

When we reached the portals of the monastery, the Abbot welcomed us. He was a tall, broad-shouldered man, about 55 years old, I should say. When he smiled he showed a set of perfect teeth. His face was kindness itself, with a forehead denoting great intelligence. His voice was deep and soft. Unfortunately he spoke only Tibetan. Yet I felt a warmth coming from him and I knew that Geshi Rimpoche had done some work on him on my behalf.

My friend was again the interpreter, but though I could catch some of it I was unable to follow the conversation completely.

I must have fallen asleep, for the next thing I felt was my friend's hand upon me saying: "We will have some supper, and then you can go to bed. In the morning we shall all meet again."

I did not eat much, as I was very tired, and then I turned into a comfortable couch in a small room off the Abbot's main bedchamber.

I did not waken till morning, and then I felt as if I had been drugged, so tired was I. Have you ever felt that healthy tiredness when all you wanted to do was to lie down and sleep, even with your clothes on? That was how I felt that night.

Chapter II

It seemed as if a whole week had been crammed into the two days at Lhasa, and meeting with Geshi Rimpoche again was just as much as I could take. I heard Geshi Rimpoche say (in Tibetan) to the Abbot: "My son is tired, he must have rest now."

I don't know when I had felt so tired, and I was indeed glad to go to sleep.

As soon as my head was on the pillow I was fast asleep and did not know anything till I heard the chonghas sounding next morning. We all had breakfast together in the Abbot's quarters and then went outside to look down to the valley far below. I really felt I could do with a day's rest here, and said so to my friend. He said: "I am pleased, because it is Geshi Rimpoche's desire that we stay one day with him now."

I asked: "What has brought him here?" My friend explained: "He is very attached to you; you are to him as a son and even more that; it was to see you again that he has travelled all this distance."

Just then he came over to where we were. He put his arm around my shoulders and asked: "Were you surprised to see me here?" I said I was overjoyed to look upon his face again. "In fact you were very much in my mind as we came up the valley yesterday, and I said so to my friend here. All I got from him was a sort of knowing smile. But when I saw you my heart leaped with joy."

I could not have said anything better. It was true, it was spontaneous from my heart, and he knew it, for I felt coming from him a sudden warm glow which went through me like electricity, and his face lit up as if the sun were shining through it. "Let us go over there and sit down," he said.

So we went over to the alcove which faced down the valley to where the Kya Chu flowed into Tobing Chu, winding its way in some part smoothly, but in other parts the water was rushing over the boulders sending a white spray up into the air.

The abbot and my friend were having an animated conversation. So we were left alone. Geshi Rimpoche said: "I do want you to have the benefit of my life's work. I want you to see all that is false, for in this way only can you find the true."

I said: "Yes, since I left you my mind has been going through a state of transformation. For I can see, now, that nothing in the mind can reveal the Truth. No idea, no experience, not even the accumulated thought of the ages past, can ever reveal the truth. "That is true, my son," he said, "all the Truth the mind can produce is merely a projection of itself and that is not the Truth."

I wished then that he would keep on talking to me on the Yoga of the Christ. He must have got my thought for he suddenly closed his eyes as he always did when speaking in this way. The he began in the magical voice and every word he said had a transforming effect upon me. I listened not to the words but listened in a way that enable me to understand myself, that self that was hiding and covering up the Real. His voice was like music as he spoke; it was like old times again. If you have read my book Beyond the Himalayas you will know what I mean.

He began with these words: "Only true meditation can reveal the Real. Although you will not know what it is, you will realise that the mind can never reveal it. The mind, the known, can never reveal the Unknown. The mind is merely ideas, memories, experiences--- that is all the mind is made up of and it can never reveal the Real Truth. What most people think is the truth is merely a projection of their mind. They may read about the Truth or they may listen to words which are merely other people's ideas, but now you know that that is not Truth. Truth can only be revealed from within, never from without.

I replied: "Yes, I have found that out when I was with you at Lingmatang. I realised now that concentration on an idea only narrows down the mind, and a mind that is narrowed down can never understand that which is limitless, immeasurable. Even prayer is not true meditation. Through repetition of words and sentences one can make the mind still and in that stillness receive a response, but that response is not the response of Reality---it is a response of the unconscious mind, because prayer is merely a begging, a supplication and can never be creative. In prayer there is always duality, one who begs and one who grants. You pray for something you haven't got, either a motor-car or a virtue and so on.

"Jesus said, in other words: When you pray believe you have received. This was the immediate present. *Everything is now.* Meditation is really finding out what the mind is made up of. Now, not some time later, but **NOW.**

"What your mind is made up of is your conditioning which is always seeking expression in thought Now! To know yourself you must be aware of your thinking Now; then there will not be a yesterday or a tomorrow. For when the mind ceases to chatter Reality is, And Reality is everpresent **NOW.**

"Yes," he went on, "true meditation means a mind that is capable of swift pliability, aware extensively and widely, and limitless, so that every problem as it arises can be dissolved instantaneously, every challenge being understood *now* in which there is no response of yesterday. True meditation is a self-revealing process. Meditation that is not self-revealing is not meditation, it is merely a contracting process that can never reveal anything."

"To know yourself," I said, "is to know all the content of the mind both the conscious and the unconscious activities---when it is awake and when it is in its so-called sleep. You have shown me that it is not difficult, yet at times I find it disturbing."

"That is because you are looking for a result, my son," he explained. "Let us experiment now, not knowing what you are to find, and you will find always something new. Newness cannot come through memory, can it? Memory is not new is it? Meditate with me as I go along, and step by step you will be doing the same. We are experimenting to find out not tomorrow but the Living Present.

"First of all realise that meditation without self-knowledge has no meaning; self- knowledge is not high or low; your higher or your lower self is but an idea, a product of the mind which is time, and time cannot reveal the Timeless. Therefore in true meditation the concentration on the higher self does not mean a thing. Truly, meditation is to uncover the whole process of thought which is memory and this can be done immediately. Truth is *not* a matter of time; Truth is *now* or it can never be. Time can never reveal the Timeless. Memory- thought is the product of time, is it not? Now what is the self? Obviously it is memory---at whatever level, high or low, it is still memory. As I said, the idea of a higher self and a lower self is merely speculation, a product of the mind, is it not? If you look into it you will find out that it is so. The higher self and the lower self are merely ideas---something you have read somewhere--- you think about it and now you think it is real, but it is not a reality.

"You may call the higher self Atman-spirit but it is still an idea in the mind. When you call it Atman you place it at a high level, but it is still part of that which is memory. Therefore to understand the whole process of "myself" I must understand memory, ideas, thought which is the same thing. There can be no self without thought or memory. So I must understand memory which his not only acquired the previous minute or yesterday but is also the memory of centuries---memory which is the result of accumulated experience of time, all the influences of the past. All this is memory, whether on the surface or deep in the consciousness.

20

Chapter II

"But to investigate memory in every detail would take time, though time can never reveal the Truth, for the Truth is Timeless and is *now*. Therefore to use time would be useless. Most people are in the habit of using time to reveal the Timeless, but Truth to them is just as far away as ever. Now we come to the realisation that thought is the result of memory, and memory must be dissolved instantaneously.

"Now," he went on, "you see the self, the you, is but a bundle of memories which project themselves in the form of thought. Thought and the self are not separate; they are one. This can never be the Truth nor can it reveal the Truth. But we must come to that which is beyond the mind beyond memory, beyond time. *But as long as memory functions there can only be time, and time is not Reality.*"

I did not answer one way or another, for at the moment it was getting clearer and transformation was taking place ---I was seeing something I had not seen before. I could now realise that the mind was but a product of time, of memories, of ideas; I could see that, to be free, the mind must see that it can never reveal the Truth. Both conscious or unconscious, high or low, memories could not reveal that which is beyond. I could see that the mind---the me--- could never reveal the Truth. Only by ceasing to think about the Truth could I experience the Truth. When I saw this the mind became still, not a forced stillness but a stillness that came through freedom. I no longer wished to be anything. *The desire to become had vanished; my mind could never transform itself into the Truth; nor could it find the Truth.* To reveal the Truth it must be still. Then there was a stillness that was not of Time, a stillness that was not forced or compelled but a stillness that came through understanding that, when the mind ceased to chatter, in that silence was the Real, the Unknown came into being. This was Creativeness. I had no desire for a result. All action ceased, thinking ceased, and this was the highest form or thinking because no there was Creativeness. My thought was no longer the expression of memory, of the past, of what I thought was true or what not true. I saw things as they are, and was no longer caught up in them. All intellectual activity stopped. I no longer wandered or wondered. Now there was neither the thought nor the thinker, neither the experience nor the experiencer. There was no experience now through memory, through time. There was only a state of experiencing in which time had vanished. Yesterday, today, tomorrow had completely stopped; they did not really exist except in the mind. The mind no longer caught up in time was without time, and that which is without time is eternal with no beginning, no ending, without cause, and therefore without effect and that which is without cause is Real. The Father performs His own deeds. Here was Creativeness---Completeness.

I saw now that the Truth was immediate, the mind, the product of time, had completely stopped. Immediately I saw that all thought was of time, every human problem now could be solved, not in time but now, for Reality had no problem. Only man created his own problems, and to know this was the way to solve them.

I could see that all human problems were the result of memory, of experience, of time. I knew that memory could not solve them; they could not be solved on their own level. It was when memory ceased they were solved *now at once.* They did not exist in the Timeless; only in time did they exist, and time did not exist except in the mind where the problem existed. When God is and there is nothing else, all human problems dissolve away in Love and Wisdom-God.

When I saw this, Creativeness came into being and I knew that all was well. Infinity was the only Reality. I was not a mere automaton but an active Creative Principle that existed everywhere and having no beginning, therefore no ending. Now I knew what the knowledge of the self meant. The self did not exist in Reality, and knowing this I knew Reality was liberation.

So *now* is the only time. There is no tomorrow, no yesterday---when these cloud the present, the now is not realised. So meditation is not a means of concentration, which is contraction, exclusion and limitation. Meditation is Freedom, Freedom from time.

Now I knew that there was only One---the Ever New. There was no duality, no opposition, no desires, no cravings, no past, no future, all that was of the mind, that was the me that lived in separation. The Father and I were one, the Yoga of the Christ was the only true Yoga. The me and the mine now dissolved, only the Whole was real: the drop became the ocean. I knew now what the Master meant when he said, "The Father and I are one." It was not an idea but Reality. Thinking could never create the Real, because thinking was of time; neither could thinking reveal the Timeless. I knew this now. Only when thinking the product of memory ceased; when that which continued came to an end, the Everlasting came into Being.

In this silence that was not created there was Being, freed from memory, freed from time, moment to moment was the Ever-present-Now.

I knew now that there was no higher self or lower self; that also was division, a mere mental creation. No matter at what level, this self was merely an idea, for the idea of time was an illusion.

Just then my friend and the Abbot came over to us and sat down beside us. My friend said: "We waited till we saw you both coming back into the world of time before we disturbed you."

"You know," he said, "this is one of Geshi Rimpoche's favourite sanctuaries. He will be waiting for you here when you return from Zamsar and you will go back together to Lingmatang. We could not now let you go alone."

I replied: "There could not be anything I would like better."

23

Chapter II

The remainder of the morning drifted by with general conversation about Lhasa and Potala. It was soon noon and a Lama came out to say that food was waiting for us. I wondered what it would be like and was greatly impressed to find lovely barley broth and mutton beautifully cooked, delicious bread made from barley meal and fresh butter, and of course, Tibetan tea. I had got used to this tea by now and liked it, though at first it tasted to me like castor oil. Tea, yak butter, salt and boiling water made up the tea, a wonderful mixture!

Geshi Rimpoche had already told the Abbot all about me and he said, in Tibetan, "I wish I could speak your language. I would like to hear all about your work and where you have been." Funnily enough I found that I could keep up a fair conversation in Tibetan; even though I could not get the accent on certain words, he could understand me. When our conversation finished, both my friend and Geshi Rimpoche clapped their approval of my Tibetan conversation.

During the afternoon we made a tour of the monastery. In all there were about 500 Lamas in Tragtse monastery. The front of the monastery was right out on the edge of the rock face; a sheer drop to the valley would be over 1,000 feet. The building of the monastery must have been a herculean task. The temple hall had large trunks of trees to hold up the roof. "How did they get them up?" I asked.

"All by hand," he replied, "pulled up from the valley by many willing hands with several ropes at a time tied on to the one tree. The big boulders were hewn and blasted out of the rock face. You know the Tibetan builders are perhaps the best in the world for this kind of work."

All monasteries are much the same, the uniqueness of this being that it was built high up on the rock face of the mountain. Down in the valley, just in front of the monastery, the Kya Chu ran into the

24

Robing Chu. Just here the water made a roaring noise like an express train, as it rushed over the great boulders.

The track we would take in the morning ran along the Kya Chu. We were now just two days' journey away from Zamsar.

It was a refreshing day and I felt replenished for the last stage of the journey. I was anxious to see my friend's sanctuary about which I had heard so much.

That night I slept just as soundly as I did the previous night and felt as if I could do the two days' journey in one day. I said so to my friend but he smiled and said: "It is a good thirty miles, my son, and the going is rough; you will have to walk a good part of the way, for there are some very dangerous places, and it would not be advisable to take them on the back of your pony."

We started off about six o'clock in the morning, and we planned to reach a place called Dechen Dzong that night, and the next night to reach Zamsar. Our ponies were housed down in the valley in stables belonging to the monastery, so we said *au revoir* happily, as we would meet again. Going down the rock face steps with our haversacks full of food was an even more difficult task than going up. We got on our ponies and off we went. I felt exhilarated as I breathed the fresh morning breeze and saw the water rushing over the big boulders sending white spray in all directions; besides, the wonderful, majestic scenery was a tonic in itself.

Few, if any, Westerners had gone beyond Lhasa, and so I felt a sense of importance at my accomplishments up to the present.

CHAPTER III

We had just gone a short distance from Tragste Gompa (Gompa means monastery) when we came across a magnificent waterfall. The river pass here through a narrow gorge; the water shot out fifth feet before it turned downwards, and the noise was deafening. As it reached halfway down, the water fell on to another ledge, from where it poured over into a great pool at the bottom. The track from here led up the mountainside and out to the right into a large fertile area called Zenshi, an area which was highly cultivated. Quite a number of Tibetan houses were dotted here and there in this valley through which the Kya Chu flowed.

Here we came upon some geese with black stripes over their heads from side to side, and a black stripe down the back of the neck. They looked at us and made much noise. They are called bar-headed geese, so my friend told me. There were also lots of duck, and some vultures and fish eagles called Pallas; these birds, which have long beaks slightly turned down at the end, were swooping down on the fish in the river. A great number of other kinds of birds screamed and circled over our heads.

Butterflies of all colours and sizes were also fluttering around. What a paradise, I thought; and what a chance for a collector of rare butterflies not seen in other parts of the world! Wild flowers and rhododendron trees grew where there was no cultivation. Many types of lizard were seen, one dangerous if cornered; it was a big black rock lizard about three feet long with large feet and long jaws. The surrounding scenery was superb; mountain on all sides, covered with the eternal snows.

The sun was getting hot by now and there was no breeze; but soon the wind would rise, as it always does about noon.

When we left this area we had some stiff climbing to do. At one time we would be down by the riverside, and then high up the mountainside; the trail had been fairly good for most of the way that we had already come, but I was told that there were many dangerous places. Anyway I was content, for I knew that all would be well.

A number of rivers were flowing into the Kya Chu, these came from the mountains on each side. At this time of the year the snow is melting and there is always a big flow of water. Later on, when the water comes, these rivers are frozen up. It is much easier then to cross rivers and lakes but travelling is much more difficult and dangerous in the deep snow.

We passed a number of Tibetans travelling, women and men, some on donkeys, some on yaks. Some of the trains of yaks carrying goods were on their way towards Lhasa. Yaks are used mostly in this part of the country, as they are easier to feed and more sure-footed than the donkey and can carry heavier loads.

We came across a family, father, mother and two daughters, who were known to my friend. They were travelling from Zamsar to Lhasa for the festival that was to take place there soon. All the large monasteries have big festivals about that time of the year and people came from near and far to attend them.

I was introduced to the family. The two girls were of a beautiful type of Tibetan, the Himalayan type. When they laughed their eyes sparkled, and as their beautifully formed lips smiled they showed a perfect set of teeth, I spoke to the elder girl in my poor Tibetan and to my astonishment she answered me in English. She told me that she attended school at Darjeeling and that her name was Norbu, which means precious jewel, quite a common name in Tibet. When I told her I knew another Norbu almost as pretty as herself she blushed to the roots of her hair. She said that she would return as soon as possible so that she could "talk more English". She was probably the only person in Zamsar except my friend who could speak English. She would have come back with us, but my friend said in Tibetan that we had much work to do in the meantime, though when she returned she could renew my acquaintance. So they continued on their way to Lhasa and we went on towards Zamsar. Several times she looked back at us and waved before we passed out of sight.

I said to my friend: "That is a beautiful girl!"

"Yes," he said, "she is a Tibetan beauty, no doubt. Her features are entirely different from those of the district here. The features of the people in this district are broad and with flat noses spread all over the face as it were, while the features of those in and around Yatung, where she comes from, are chiselled and finely formed."

The women in Tibet are different from all other Eastern women. They are not shy in any way and never take a back seat like their other Eastern sisters. They engage in conversation equally with their menfolk; they are open and free, and this is what makes them delightfully different.

We reached a place called Tangkya about 2.30 in the afternoon, our first stop. Here we had lunch. We could not stay more than a few minutes because we had to reach Dechen Dzong before dark, as it is very dangerous to travel then, some parts being rough and dangerous even in the daytime. We had at least four hours of travelling to do and were naturally anxious to get on.

We could travel only Indian fashion, one following the other. My friend always insisted on taking the lead and I came on immediately behind. We were still travelling along the Kya Chu.

After we left Tangkya the path led along the side of the river for a few miles, the longest stretch yet. In parts the river was smooth and deep; in other parts the water flowed over big boulders which had rolled down from the mountains. This is a very common occurrence and we had to be on the look-out all the time. Should we hear a rumbling noise we knew we must get out of the way or take shelter. It is mostly goats or wild yaks that loosen up the stones which loosen more stones on their way down.

We met some sheep carrying small loads on their backs. It is quite common to see sheep carry loads in Tibet especially from the salt lakes. Salt lakes exist in Tibet as high as 15,000 feet above sea level.

After several miles along the riverside I thought it was too good to be true, and then suddenly we came to an abrupt stop, an almost perpendicular climb up the mountainside facing us. Half-way up my friend stopped and got off his pony. I did the same. Here a part of the track had actually fallen away down into the river below. There seemed no way across this landslide. I was not worried. It was a fresh slide, looking as if it had happened only a few minutes before we came along. I asked: "And what do we do now?"

"We will turn back for about half a mile and then take the other track, the one you saw on the side of the mountain stream," he replied. "There is another track higher up, that is our only chance now."

We turned back to the point he mentioned. He then tore a prayer flag down and wrote on it with a piece of black chalk that he carried, so that others coming along would not walk into danger.

"I know now why it is necessary to get to our destination before dark," I remarked.

We climbed up the bed of the stream till we reached a track about a quarter of a mile higher up. This track came over the mountain from the other side.

"How did you know of this track?" I inquired.

Chapter III

"There is not a track in these parts that I do not know, I have come this way so often. This is not the first time that this has happened," he replied.

We kept on this track which was quite good, for about three or four miles, and then we struck the old path leading down again to the riverside. From here all the way to Dechen it was easy going and we arrived there at seven o'clock, just as it was getting dusk.

It was not long before a crowd gathered round us. I wondered what was the matter but it was just a welcome to my friend who is a great benefactor to the people of Dechen Dzong. We went to a pretty Tibetan house on the hillside, where a clear stream of water passed the side of the house. There were many prayer flags all around it I remember, for I remarked on this.

My friend said: "This is the headman of the district; his name is Iamtso. The house is very comfortable and we can rest here for the night. "As we dismounted from our ponies the door opened and a very pleasant Tibetan came running over to us; he took my friend's hands and kissed the palms, the greatest token of respect one could give in Tibet.

Supper was soon laid by his wife and we had mutton, barley bread, potatoes and Tibetan tea, and later some Tibetan beer made from barley. We sat up till about eleven o'clock listening to Iamtso playing a string instrument which he himself had made. He was a master at it. The melodies he played were so fascinating that I wanted more, but my friend said: "I think we had better get some rest now, for tomorrow means another strenuous day."

The couch I slept on was made of bamboo and yak-hide, and in a more comfortable bed I had not slept since I left the hermitage of Ling-Shi-La.

Chapter III

When I awakened in the morning I could smell breakfast cooking, yak steak and eggs, barley bread and Tibetan tea. We fed well and were off after saying our good-byes and promising to stay on our way back.

Iamtso made us take with us a whole chicken (cooked), some hard-boiled eggs and barley bread for food on the way. We did not want to take it but Iamtso was emphatic about it. So we were off again, this time on the last part of our journey to Zamsar. I was happy, knowing what was in store for me for the next few weeks. We travelled along the river for about five miles, when we came to a crossing. Here we crossed in a coracle to the other side, as the track now ran along the other side of the river to Zamsar. We went another two miles and had our lunch by the riverside. The side of the river was covered with wild flowers, and the mountainside on both sides of the river was covered with rhododendron bushes in full bloom, a sight I shall never forget. I said that I would like to live here always. My friend smiled at me and I know now why, because when I saw his sanctuary beside the Kya Chu it simply took my breath away. It was equal to Ling-Shi-La but in an entirely different setting, about which I will tell you later.

After lunch we went on our way. We reached Zamsar at the head of the Kya Chu, where numerous other rivers fed it from the various glaciers coming down between towering snowclad mountains. Around Zamsar the great Nyenchentangla Range rises to an average height of 23,000 feet, the most magnificent range of mountains beyond the Himalayas. What a sight for the gods! I would not have missed it for anything. Now I know why my friend lived in this far-away magnificent place. It was beyond description.

He pointed out the various mountains to me by name, and their height. As you looked at one the next seemed even more beautiful; the grandeur was magnificent. These towering mountains seemed so near you, you felt as if they might be falling upon you. Zamsar itself is 14,000 feet above sea level.

On the mountainside I could see a white building standing out by itself, a study in pure Tibetan architecture. As I got nearer I could see wild flowers, rhododendron bushes in full bloom, large palm trees and a highly cultivated garden with blue and yellow chinese poppies, gentian, senecio and other flowers all in full bloom.

From the river near by a canal was made which carried water right along to the house. An irrigation scheme was laid throughout, and this also fed a pond filled with lilies. Another larger pool was also filled with running water. Farther up there were some thermal springs, and from here hot water was led to the larger pool for bathing; it was also led into the house. "I could stay here forever," I exclaimed. "This is where I would like to end my earthly life. Put it down in the Western world and it would command the attention of millions of people. Money could not buy such a wonderful place."

Yes, I raved about it to my friend, who said: "It is yours, You can have it for the remainder of your life. I have given it to you *now*." For a while I could not speak. Then I said: "But how can I remain here when I have work to do?"

He answered: "The time will come when you may return." "In the physical?" I asked. "Yes," he said, "in the physical."

Perhaps in the future I may return, but at present I do not see the way opening yet. Who knows, though, what is going to happen? No one knows. At least I knew that by now.

I said: "So many unexpected things have happened, this may also happen." To have a sanctuary to go to in this, the loveliest spot in the world! Yes, Zamsar was more than I ever expected.

"Is all this true?" I felt constrained to ask. "You are not playing with me, are you?"

"No, my son, how could I, for I have followed you all your life. My life is your life, your life is my life. How could it be otherwise?"

Tears welled up in my eyes and I swallowed my saliva to hold my emotion in check! He saw this and put his arm around my shoulders and said: "I have waited many years for this day when you would be with me here and I could keep you with me. But I can see it cannot be at present, for there are higher forces than you and me behind this work. It will be hard to part with you, but you must go back into the world you came from till your work is done. God will protect you and keep you safe, for the Life that gave you birth into this world will never fail you."

With these words we went inside. The front door led into a hall where priceless tapestries were hung. Some very large priceless ancient Chinese vases stood on the floor, which was of polished wood. The walls were panelled in polished woodwork of exquisite alcoves curtained with rich brocade.

On the floor in the central room was a rich Chinese embossed carpet and in the alcoves there were rich Tibetan carpets, tables in some and couches in others. At the back of this room were other private rooms, suitably furnished as bed-sitting rooms, all self-contained.

The kitchen and out-houses were detached, and there was an air-tight larder in which meat kept fresh for weeks.

The cold atmosphere made refrigeration an easy problem.

I had a wash and clean up in the warm water which was led to the house from the thermal spring. After that we had supper which had been prepared for us.

I was shown my special quarters, one of the self-contained alcoves. My friend knew I was tired and that I should be pleased to go to bed. I did so, and slept in a deep slumber till the morning.

The sun was just rising when I awoke. I went on to the front steps. The beauty of the scene cannot be told in words. The front of the sanctuary faced the rising sun whose rays were reflected in all colours from the snowclad mountains close at hand, from deep red to yellow mingling with the blue sky. The glittering drops of dew that covered the colourful wild flowers sparkled with the reflection of the sun's rays. All this was truly a sight for the gods.

For breakfast we had some yak steak and fried eggs, with barley bread and fresh butter. My friend said: "We will not waste any time. Write down all the questions you want to ask so that you will not forget them, and we will discuss them as we go along."

This I did and there were many of them. But as we went along I had all the answers without my asking!

His words came back to me like a flash. "It does not matter very much whether it is true or not, does it?" I knew now that what I had before I came was merely my own mental creations or those of another. Much had been done since then, my mind had been completely transformed, for I knew that what was made up in my mind was not the real, it was merely a fabrication of it.

CHAPTER IV

We sat down at a table in the front hall, with the door open and looking right on to the great mountains. I was ready to begin our work. My friend looked at me and said:

"I am not going to fill you mind with ideas---that would be a hindrance to the revealing of the Real. You have pass through all the Yoga systems and you have acquired a great deal of knowledge of psychic development. But our work now is of an entirely different nature. We will call it the Yoga of the Christ, though names mean nothing, but for the benefit of others we will give it a name.

"First of all you must understand the problem of time. This must be thoroughly understood. When I say there is no time, that is a truth. There is only time in the mind of man but in Reality there is no time.

"However, in this world we have to have the time of the clock, the day, the week, month and year and so on. This is merely to enable you to keep your appointments or to make your appointments. You could not be sure of catching your train, your ship or organise at the office if there were no such time. So we will call that chronological time. Then there is another kind of time which we will call time of the mind which is the past, the future, memories, thoughts, a belief that in time you will become free and so on. This we will call psychological time. Now, it is this time we must understand, otherwise there can be no realisation of Reality because Reality---the Timeless---can never be realised through time.

"Memory is in time, your thought are the result of time, your experiences also are the result of time.

"Memories, what are they? They are the result of your experiences in time. What others have told you, your ideas, your beliefs and all that your mind is made up of---that is psychological time.

"You want Truth, but Truth is not the result of time nor can it be realised through an idea, a belief, or through time; all these things hinder the realisation of the Truth. Truth cannot come into being when these things cover It up. It can come into being only when It is uncovered, freed from time.

"The first lesson I gave you when I met you in the flesh in Kalimpong was about meditation, and this morning I am going to deal with it again for it is very important when we are seeking Truth. Meditation of the right kind is therefore essential, but few people know it. In your first lesson on Yoga you were shown how to meditate by concentrating on an idea to the exclusion of everything else. Now I am going to prove to you that this kind of meditation can never reveal the Truth. I am not saying that by this method you would not get a result but Truth is not a result. The result will still be mental and not Truth. You understand that, don't you?"

"Yes," I replied, "I do understand."

"To find out what is right meditation", he continued, "we must understand the whole process of thinking. Now, your thinking is the result of what you know. You can't think on that which you do not know; your thinking then is confined to the mind and what the mind knows and it will still be a mental thing or a conclusion, but this is not Truth. You understand that, don't you?"

"Yes, I do understand that. I see that Truth cannot be a conclusion or an idea or any mental formulation, because I create these myself, but Truth is not created because Truth is *now* and is not subject to time nor can Time reveal it. We do not create that which is now. We may speculate about it but that is not It."

"Right," he said, "what I am doing now is making you

understand yourself because without understanding the self---the me---the I or whatever you call it---there can be no revealing of Truth. The me---the I---memory, thinking and other things, which are all of the mind, must come to an end before the Real is experienced.

"Now, you have found, when you meditate through concentration, that your thought wanders, there is always a conflict. This is because you have chosen a central idea or thought to dwell upon. But this is exclusion; you are excluding everything else except this central thought, and by so doing you think you are going to find the Real, but this is impossible. Besides, you will notice that your mind wanders off repeatedly and there is a constant struggle to keep your mind focused on this central thought that you have chosen. I am not saying that concentration is not good for the mind but, as regards realising the Truth, it is a wrong process. So therefore you must have a right means at the beginning to have the right ending because they are one, are they not?"

"Yes," I said, "I see that clearly."

"Now, do not be making ideas out of what I am saying," he said; "what is essential is that you understand the whole process of the mind and how it formulates ideas."

"Again," he said, "why do you choose a central idea to concentrate on?" Is it not because you feel it will give you a reward? That is why you dwell on it; you want a result, but the Truth is not a result, so this means is not the right means.

"Now you will see if you look into your mind that there is a battle going on between the thought you chose and other thoughts that try to get expression. You may continue to concentrate and conquer all the other movements but you have not revealed the Truth, have you? If you say that one thought is right and the other wrong, it is futile. What you should find out is why the mind wanders. Why does it wander? Can you tell me?"

Well," I replied, "it is because most thoughts have not been understood. Every thought has some significance, some value, some hidden meaning, and so, like weeds, they keep coming up and the more you try to forget them the more active you make them. It is like pressing a lid down on a boiling pot."

"Yes," he said, "that shows some understanding. But that is not the complete answer to the problem. If you can look at each thought as it arises without prejudice, without fear or condemnation, look at it freely and not resist it, not push it away but uncover its meaning, then these thoughts will never come up again, they are finished with.

"The thoughts in your mind cannot affect Reality because Reality is beyond mind, and when you understand this you free the mind, and by freeing the mind it becomes quiet, and in that quietness is Reality revealed, because Reality is not made up in the mind, Reality is beyond mind, and the mind must become quiet before Reality comes into being.

"So the important thing is not controlling or contracting your thoughts but understanding them. But you cannot understand through resistance. Concentration is a narrowing down of the mind and is not the revealing process which alone frees the mind. Yet most people call this meditation which is merely a process of self-isolation, and isolation is self-protection; and a mind that is protecting itself must be full of fear. Now, how can a mind that is fearful be open to that which is Real, which is without fear?

"If you examine and understand your mental creations you will see that they are the result of your thoughts, memories, experiences, so there can be no separation between the thinker and his thoughts--- one is the product of the other. When you see clearly that the thinker is not separate from his thought you will find freedom, for they are your own creations; there is no longer a battle between the thought and the thinker, which is the cause of all your mental conflict and as you become aware of this the mind becomes quiet, there is no longer any conflict between the thinker and the thought, but there is an understanding of the whole process of thought which is self-knowledge. You understand, don't you?"

"Yes," I said, "I see when the mind is no longer forced to be quiet it becomes quiet because friction has ceased. The mind lives only in the known and the known can never reveal the unknown. When it knows that it can never know, it ceases to chatter, and becomes open to that which is beyond. I can also see that a narrow mind is a petty mind and its idea of God will also be petty, just according to its conditioning."

"Now," he went on, "the mind is becoming freed from conflict, is it not?" "Yes," I replied, "there is a sense of quietness that did not exist before."

"Well," he said, "Truth is *not* a matter of time, Truth is now, or never, and only when the mind is quiet, not forced to be quiet, is this realised. When forced to be quiet it will still be in conflict, but when it is quiet through understanding itself, then the *Truth is.* There is now no duality of the thought and the thinker or the experience and the experiencer, but only experience in which there is no duality, no resistance. Jesus said, in other words, 'It is the Father who ever remaineth in me, He doeth the work. I am nothing.'

"You may reason in the highest level, you may say that God is Infinite in nature, that there cannot be anything outside Him, that He must be everywhere, that there can be no substance except His, no life except His, no creativeness apart from Him, otherwise He could not be infinite. Yet this reason must cease for the very fact that the mind is trying to convince itself of the fact; the mind is still formulating and, although helpful, does not reveal the Truth that is beyond mind. Even the highest thought has to cease because thought can never reveal the Truth.

"So the process of understanding oneself is the beginning of meditation. There is no special technique, no special posture, no acquired method of breathing.

"For without knowing yourself, which is mind, whatever you think has no reality, no real basis. You can see that, can't you?"

"Yes," I said, "I see that clearly now."

"Now to know yourself there must be constant awareness moment to moment without compulsion, without condemnation or justification---just a passive alertness in which you see things as they are. Then there is no problem, the problem has ceased to be because you---the mind---are the problem. Reality has no problem; only the mind of man that is in confusion has a problem. When confusion ceases, then the problem does not exist. Reality alone exists, all else is illusion. In that perfect tranquillity, in this stillness of the heart and mind *Reality is.* This is the Yoga of the Christ. It is the Father and He alone is the Real. His operation is wide, extensive, unlimited and perfect.

"Now," he said, "to meditate you need *no* method or system, because that creates a pattern and Truth is not a pattern. The right means in the beginning must be freedom so that freedom will be. Now take an hour by yourself and discern every thought as it rises, then you will know yourself."

In my meditation I saw clearly that the mind could never reveal the truth, so it was no longer agitated, no longer struggling for a result. Then I knew that Reality was now, it was not a matter of time, now was the Timeless. I felt as if I were giving expression to the

Unknown. Although sensation was not necessary, in fact often a hindrance, I felt my body being lifted from the couch upon which it lay.

What I did know now was that Truth was *immediate,* it was not a matter of time, that in memory including the memory of every entity for centuries past could never reveal the Real. I knew all the searching, all evolutionary process of time, could not reveal Reality. Yet I knew it was *now,* for time had dissolved away; time was a product of my mind, my mind was the product of time, all the learning, all the intellectual words or ideas, could not reveal Reality, because Truth was beyond all the phases of mind, high or low, and no matter what the mind could think, that could not be Reality. Only when my mind ceased to chatter, in that silence my livingness was revealed, the only Real was my Livingness, that was neither a memory nor an idea. I did not know what it was but I knew that it was. To know what it was would be to put it in time, and that was impossible. I could understand the Master now. I knew now why he spoke in parables because he could not reveal the Real to others, for everyone must find It by himself/herself and alone.

This was the Yoga of the Christ, the greatest of all Yoga. You do not do anything of your own accord; the self dissolves and is no longer a hindrance to the Real. It was the Father who was Eternal, the only Real, He did the work. This was the only way to solve all problems, to see them for what they were, for they could not be solved on their own level. In trying to do so we only create more problems. What is necessary is to remove the cause and the cause is the self with all its intrigue, greed, desire for position and power. The foundation of the existence of the self is separation which is perpetuating and increasing all our problems, and if you look into yourself you will see that you are the root of the problem. We blame everything and everyone else but ourselves; yet we are responsible for the conditions in which we live.

Chapter IV

To destroy property and kill people, then to give them food and clothing as a means of solving the problem is an illusion. Only when we see clearly what we are doing does the problem dissolve. The problem is ourselves, therefore to understand the self with all its memory, experience, greed, desire, believing, wanting and not wanting, ideas and ideals, when we see these as they are, not merely thinking around them, then and then only does the self, which is the cause of the problem, understand the problem. Reality has no problem; only man has.

It was lunch time when I arose. There was no need for me to say a word; my friend knew, and he saw for himself a greater light than ever before. It was now for me to be consciously aware just as Jesus was, when he said, "Get thee behind me, Satan." This was the satan of the self, not some theological concoction outside oneself, but the self that always wants to be in front. And if you look into the self, if you are aware, you will see how it is always the self that wants to be in front. But when you know the self, then freedom from the self comes, and not before. "Get thee behind me, Satan." In other words, I am nothing, the Father alone is real. Yes, the self is the deceiving element, there is no doubt about that.

No remarks were made. The wisdom of my friend was complete, and I felt content with a freedom that was not the result of any stimulation or self-hypnosis but a freedom that comes through understanding.

After lunch we put our climbing boots on and went up the valley of the Nyiblung Richung, the name of the peak right in front of us. The glacier in this valley was not more than a few miles away. We could hear the crunching noise as this great river of ice forced its way down. When we reached the edge of the glacier we could see great crevasses, big enough to swallow a house.

Many mountains surround Zamsar and my friend pointed out the various peaks, detailing their heights from 20,000 to 24,000 feet.

Nature was unadorned in all her beauty, a beauty that no other Westerner had ever set eyes upon. When Jesus looked upon the lilies of the field he said, "Solomon in all his glory was not arrayed like one of these."

My friend told me some of his experiences of climbing these mountains. He described the best route to take with a feeling of satisfaction of accomplishment. I knew that feeling, for I had done a lot of climbing myself.

I can remember, when I was climbing in the southern Alps, that I thought I would take a short cut on the way down, only to find myself on the top of a precipice of ice and rock, impossible to descend, and I had no alternative but to go back the way I came. I wasted a few hours in doing so, as well as making others anxious.

The feeling you have when you come upon a snag can be understood only when experienced.

"What is the height of that peak?" I asked.

"Twenty-three thousand feed," replied my friend.

"Do you think we could climb it one day?" I asked. (The climbing bug was getting hold of me again.)

"No," he said, "this peak has never been climbed yet. Several have made attempts and failed.

"Later on, perhaps," he replied, with a challenging look at the towering peak that had resisted all attempts, up to now.

The challenge also kept cropping up in my mind all the way down.

I said: "I am going to bring up my camera with my six-inch telephoto lens and I will take a number of pictures, perhaps we may find a spur and climb round that mushroom top."

I could see through his field glasses that the top was like a mushroom, and how to get above that mushroom formation was the difficulty we had now to overcome.

"That was the cause of the failure of every attempt," he said. This made me all the more eager to have a try.

I don't know if you ever had the climbing bug accentuated in you, but when it does get under your skin it is a fascinating urge that make you try and try again.

We returned that evening just as the sun was beginning to set and we sat watching the changing of colour. The sun now was behind us and we were facing the mountain. As the sun went down, the pink glow on the clouds became darker until it got to a dark purple. This changing of colour was fascinating. More clouds began to gather in the valley and were creeping up the mountainside, gradually hiding it till only the top of the peak covered in snow stood out, reflecting the rays of the sun in all the colours of the rainbow. They sky gradually became darker blue, and the twinkling stars began to appear like sparkling diamonds on the blue canopy above us, as the blanket of clouds began covering the snow peaks as if putting them to sleep.

After supper, which I relished, for I was hungry after our trail up the valley, and the freshness of the air had sharpened my appetite, my friend produced pictures of the various climbs he had made and described them in detail. It was queer how fascinating those pictures were to me, and I wished that I had some of my own with me, pictures that I had taken years ago.

Chapter IV

After an hour or so I asked if we were going to do more work that night, for I was eager to hear him again. But he said, no, I had done enough for one day. "Tomorrow morning when you are fresh we will renew our work."

There was a real affinity between us; we could talk or be quiet; there was never a moment that seemed out of place. With most people, even your nearest relations, there are moments that tax you, but here the harmony was beyond anything I had ever known before, and this lasted throughout the whole period I was there.

What I seemed to want was always there, always done; his desire was always in accord with me, and my desire was always in accord with his. His greater wisdom was a joy to me. His guidance was smooth and easy, and I grew to love him more and more and to admire his great understanding. We were twin souls and when I said this to him he replied: "That is why I chose you, my son."

"A truly wonderful experience for me," I said.

To absorb the wisdom of such a master was indeed a great privilege, yet he always made me feel that he was just like myself.

I retired for the night and did not awake until the gong sounded as the sun rose, which was the regular custom.

CHAPTER V

EACH morning was different.

It had rained in the valley through the night and the mountains were covered with more snow. There was a thin mist which the fresh wind was blowing away. The sun was beginning to peep through. It was like a morning in the Highlands of Scotland, the only difference being that the mountains were much bigger and more rugged, and the scenery more gigantic.

My friend had already been down to the village. He was the great helper; everyone looked to him for help and understanding. They were indeed lucky people.

I said to him as he came up the steps: "You had an early start this morning."

"Yes," he remarked, "I have just delivered a baby boy to the headman's wife early this morning, about three o'clock, and both are doing well. In two days she will be about again." This was a new phase of life I saw him in, and marvelled at his all-round capabilities.

"Yes," he said, "many of the children you see around here have been delivered by me, so I am quite an expert hand by now."

"Have you had breakfast?" he asked.

"No," I replied, "I have just got up, shaved and washed, and had a dip in the pool," which was quite warmed up with the water from the hot spring. "In fact I was waiting for you. I wondered where you had disappeared to."

"Yes," he said, "I have been on the job since two o'clock this morning, and I just went down again to see how things were. Everything is perfect."

Chapter V

I said, "The mortality among newly born babies in Tibet must be heavy." "Yes," he replied, "but not in this district; we have lost very few."

"By the number of children around," I remarked, "I can see that must be so. All due to your wonderful gift of healing and love."

"Lets have breakfast," he said, as if to break off my praise and admiration.

He always made me realise that within everyone is the Spirit of God, but that in most it is cluttered up with religious dogma, beliefs and other distractions of the mind. "These things I do, greater things shall ye do if you will but understand," he said. "Similar words were said nearly two thousand years ago, but people have not progressed very much since then, mainly because they are imitators of the blind."

"You must not worship any image or any so-called representation of the Christ in stone, wood or in human form," he went on, "for that will lead you away from the Christ within, they become the tools of the false prophets who control, cajole and exploit them. Only when they become enlightened can they free themselves from this bondage."

After a pause I broke off and said: "There is nothing I would like better this morning than a glass of milk for breakfast."

"All right, my son, you shall have it."

Yak milk is rich in butterfats, the cream is delicious, and I had some with my porridge most mornings. This particular morning I just wanted a glass of milk.

After breakfast we went into the front hall which faced the mountain, With this scene and atmosphere I always felt keenly alert.

Chapter V

"This morning I am going to speak to you on hope," he said. Then he began in that tone of voice that I knew so well: "Hope is a state of uneasiness. When there is a state of incompleteness man lives in hope. The prophet says in Proverbs 17, verse 10, 'A reproof entereth more into a wise man than a hundred stripes into a fool.' A wise man recognises the error but a foolish man repeats it.

"Most people, in fact nearly all, are searching for outward security. But when there is outward insecurity there is always inward insecurity, and when there is inward insecurity there must be outward insecurity, because the inward is always expressing itself outwardly. With this lack of understanding mankind has developed a philosophy of hope.

"Now the man who clings to hope is a dying man; he is not living, because to him what is important is the future, not what *is now.* Therefore a man who lives in hope is not living at all. He is living somewhere in the future, and living in the future is not living *now,* but now is the only time, for now is the only Real; you cannot live yesterday or tomorrow. If you live in the future or in the past you are merely living in your mind, then Life is merely an idea, living in Time which is but an illusion.

"Most people think in terms of opposites; they seek a state in which there is no disturbance. Why? Merely because they are disturbed. Now if this is so with you, you must find out why the mind is disturbed, then you will understand why you hope.

"The moment you are uncertain you fall into a state of hopelessness, and then you develop a philosophy of hope. But when you see the truth about hope there comes freedom from both hopelessness and hope.

"Is it not a fact that before you began to understand yourself you were afraid of not being something; that was when you did not discern the fact that the thought and the thinker were not separate and you looked at your thought distinct from the thinker, and thus you feared the thought. But you see now that the thought creates the thinker and the thinker thinks around it, so they are not separate.

"You must strip yourself of all this conditioned thought by seeing how it comes about. How does it come about? Can you tell me?"

"Well," I said, "It comes about through response to memory and environment, both inherited and acquired."

"Yes," he observed, "the self must discern its own ways, for the self and the thought are one and the same. When this is understood there is tranquillity.

"You will see now that the self has no reality; it is merely a bundle of memories and experiences which are being continually projected, so the self is caught up in its own thought- experiences and this makes up the mind. You can see now that all this is of the mind; and when this is not discerned and understood, there is fear; and because you are afraid you hope. So hope and fear are opposites in the mind, and there can be no revealing of the Real that is ever-present. While this conditioning remains the Living Presence is not realised.

"When the past and the future are dissolved in the present through understanding there is tranquillity, and in that tranquillity there is the Real, the very livingness that is creative. The Creativeness is always in the present, in the *now,* and never in the future or the past; so you see how stupid it is to develop a philosophy or hope."

"Yes," I concurred, "I can see now that my mind is being transformed, fears that I had have passed. I inherited ideas of right and wrong, what is spiritual and what is not spiritual, but I know they are merely ideas, and while I feared one I accepted the other. But spirituality is Love, Wisdom and Kindliness; these come only when conflict has dissolved through understanding."

"Yes," he said, "you built around you conclusions which you called understanding; and now you see that these conditions are a hindrance to understanding, a hindrance to the understanding of your conditioning.

"So through fear you clung to a ritual through which you tried to escape, so you were further conditioned. Your conclusions became a wall that you built around yourself; you were imprisoned, and while you were in a prison of your own making you built up and tore down, contrasting and modifying, suppressing and renewing, which merely created more confusion, which was but a projection of the self from within its own prison with its fears, its contra- dictions. Only through seeing the self, what the self is undergoing, can this conditioning be dissolved. Only in this way can the self free itself from its own illusion.

"When the self is seen merely as a bundle of memories, experiences, limitations, beliefs, conformities, only then is there freedom from this self-enclosure. When the self sees why it struggles, agitation ceases, and in that tranquillity is the Real, the Life, that is eternal, wide and unlimited in its operation. When the consciousness is freed it realises that it was always free except when it accepted the illusion of time, of memory, of experience, past and future; only in living in the present is there freedom. Therefore, when we discern the illusion moment to moment, it dissolves into its native nothingness and in this awareness the Real is--- the Creative comes into being.

"When the self was imprisoned it prayed to a God outside, that is why the believer will never know God---the Unknown---and since

53

most people believe in a God outside themselves they will never know God. But the non-believer in God, which is but another form of belief, also hinders the discovery of the Unknown---because belief and non-belief are but a response to conditioning. Belief is the result of the known, it is part of the known, which is memory, and memory can never realise the Unknown.

"Memory says, 'I do not know God, it is something unknown." So memory creates the Unknown and then believes in it as a means of experiencing the Unknown, but you will see that this is just a mental fabrication that has no substance. It is only when the mind is free from its own fabrications can the Unknown be discovered, and this discovering comes from within and not from without."

"I can see now," I said, "that conclusions are a hindrance to understanding because the self is caught up in them. They become the central image of the self and so blind it, being caught up in the illusion."

"Yes," he continued, "conclusion and the self are not separate. When this is understood there is transformation and release, there is a dropping of all conclusions. So the mind becomes infinitely pliable and only in an infinitely pliable mind is the Real discovered.

"From conclusions we form resolutions. Resolutions are stupid; they are merely a suppression of desire, and with suppression there can be no understanding. When you are watchful in the present you will find the ramifications of the mind, at the different layers. The ways of the self are laid bare. To be jealous in any layer, high or low, is to be bound by jealousy.

"From the mere superficial envy to the more subtle forms in the mental and spiritual is also a hindrance to the Creativeness within.

"*Creativeness is a state of Being that is not the outcome of*

54

thinking. It is the outcome of transformation through understanding what is false.

"In our relation to things, to people, if we watch our reactions in this relationship we will become aware of what the self is made up of. You will see that to each reaction there is memory, fear, vanity, greed, resistance, acceptance, beliefs, etc., etc. You will see by these reactions in your relationship what you are, and to know what you are is self-knowledge and this alone leads to freedom.

"When you are alert, aware, through this awareness you will see yourself as you really are, without condemnation, without fear, without judgment, and then you will understand how the mind is made up. Then the Real which is not created will come into being. The Father does the work. The Father is ever-present everywhere in the present, the only intelligence behind all creation.

"Now, look into your mind and you will see how you have been conditioned, influenced by the thoughts of others, by leaders in religious, political and economic fields of exploitation. All these are not instruments of Truth, they are the reverse. To discover Reality, which alone is Creative, you must become aware of the subtleties of influence and your response to it."

I could now understand his wisdom. I could see that the only True influence was the influence of the Spirit which was free, no longer giving expression to what the mind was made up of, but giving expression to that which was Love and Wisdom and in this was the tremendous power of right thinking, the secret of the Christ Yoga.

"Yes," I said, "I can see now why the world is in a mess."

"Yes, but the clearing of the mess begins with you and me; don't look outside yourself for the cause."

Chapter V

"Yes," I commented, "when the past ceases to influence the present, then only can Creativeness be experienced. It is when the mind is understood with all its contradictions and limitations that it becomes still. Then that which is beyond the mind will come into being, then the 'I' will have lost itself in the Infinite 'One.'"

"When there is a desire to become, a desire to achieve a result," he explained, "there must be a contradiction, and where there is contradiction there cannot be a quiet mind that is essential to realising the whole significance of Life. So thought, which is the product of time, can never realise that which is Timeless, can never know that which is beyond time. The very nature of your thinking is in terms of the past and the future, and therefore can never be fully aware of the Living present, therefore cannot be completely aware of a fact in the now--- because thought, which is the product of time, tries to eliminate its opposite, its contradiction and all the problems that it itself creates. Thought merely pursues an end.

It is when the thinker and the thought come to an end through understanding what thought is, that the Real is realised."

"I can see," I said, "that if I am seeking happiness through material, mental or so-called spiritual means I am exploited. I can see that I am the cause of this exploitation. When I seek happiness external to myself I become the creator of the exploiter, whether on the material, mental or spiritual plane. The exploiter does not come into being suddenly; he is not a freak of nature, but is the result of my demands for material, mental and spiritual satisfaction in which there is no freedom and that which I seek I never attain.

"Yes," he said, "that is perfectly true, but there is a more subtle problem---what people rebel against is the result of their own actions which they call evil, and some think that by killing a few they will destroy the evil; they think that by killing and imprisoning a few who they think are responsible for the evil they will destroy the evil, but they only add to it, because they do not discern the part they play in creating it.

"Wrong means can never establish right action; there can be no peace by merely murdering those who are murderers. It means that you also become a murderer. As long as we divide ourselves into groups, nationalities, different religions, different ideologies, there will be the aggressors and the defenders; then the defenders become the aggressors. Not until man sees how he has been conditioned through ignorance and tradition, through acquisition, through ideals, through following another can there be peace and freedom.

"Evil cannot be overcome by evil or any opposing action, for that leads to further aggression and more evil. Only by understanding how this division comes about can peace come to man and the world. Peace can never be the result of aggression, peace can never come out of war, peace can come only when the causes of war---aggression, nationalities, differing religious organisations---when all these things are understood, then they can be dissolved. Then Love-God-Peace, which is not created but is Eternal and Ever-present, comes into being. You do not create peace; Love-peace is the fundamental principle of unity that existed before the world was, and is the only Reality now. 'I am the only "One", there is none other beside Me."

"Spirituality is all-inclusive in which there is no distinction, no division, no desire for position or acquisition. To remain free from this net of ignorance you must maintain the freedom of your own thoughts, refusing to become a slave to imitation and tradition or the authority of the less informed than yourself.

"The world's conception is based upon selfishness with all its subtle ramifications, its illusions, its fears, its contradictions. Man unconsciously acts through fear and becomes irresponsible and this leads to further chaos and disorder.

Chapter V

"Conscious action through understanding and adjustment leads to pure thinking, which leads to pure action in which there is no longer aggression, selfishness, hatred and murder. Only then will there be a realisation of the Presence that is Ever-present, which is never in opposition to Itself at any time in any individual, nation or group.

"You will discern that good and evil are not entities of themselves; they are simply words with which we indicate the result of our actions.

"These actions are predetermined by the character of our thinking, and the cause of this thinking is ignorance of the self in bondage. Therefore an understanding of the self is paramount in the elimination of sorrow and conflict in the world in which we live.

"To become aware of that which hinders the Christ Consciousness---the expression of Reality---is of first importance. This is your task in the world, not sweet words or ideas that maintain man's ignorance. Beliefs narrow down the mind. Only seeing things as they are, and understanding how they come about, frees the mind from bondage.

"With a clear mind capable of understanding the cause, a mind that cannot be distracted through criticism or antagonism, patriotism, religious formalities and political trickery, a mind that sees how mankind is conditioned, and in the awareness of this conditioning, it will fade away. Only in a mind that is free is there true inspiration---this is the Yoga of the Christ.

"When you pray think not that you are one and God another, nor look outside for inspiration, otherwise you will be lost in the illusion of separation. Know that there is but one Life and this Life which is yours is in your brothers and sisters. You cannot be a portion of the Infinite and your brother another, for there is no division in the One Life. Although there are many members of the one body---including your heart, your lungs, your liver, your nervous system, your bones, and your limbs---there is but one body, and the one blood serves all members in the one body.

Likewise are the different nationalities all members of the one body and the one Life in all.

"When you understand what is false, then only is there Truth, and there cannot be anything else but the Truth, for all else has no foundation of its own. It has no existence in Truth, for Truth is all there is, and there is no division in Truth. Division is the illusion of man's mind."

With these words he stopped. I remained silent; I could not do otherwise. My mind had ceased to think. I had learned the art of listening, not merely creating ideas of what he said, but listening in such a way that transformation could take place through understanding myself. I knew now that this self-knowledge was the key to wisdom and without self-knowledge there could be no wisdom.

Have you ever sat dumb during an inspiring talk? You could not repeat what was said, but what was said altered your whole life afterwards. A great change took place within and with it a sense of freedom such as you could not explain. This was the feeling I had after each talk, a sense of freedom that was always new. The bonds of the past were slipping away.

We sat there for some time, yet time to me at that moment did not exist. To me the past and the future were dissolved in the now, and now was the only time. In this deep silence was the Real. It was the all, all power in heaven and on earth was Now, and that power was Love.

It was because people did not live in the present---hope was more important to them. But when you look into the matter hope is always somewhere in the future. Yet the future is only in the mind. Your *Livingness* is always in the present, never in the past or the future. Now is creative, this very moment, and is ever new, moment to moment, in which memory is dissolved and Love becomes the only Reality.

Perhaps you have experienced such a moment; so wonderful was it that you try to recapture it, but by trying to recapture the moment that is past you can never experience the moment that is *Now*. The moment that was past is an experience, a memory. The past and the future do not exist except in your mind. But *now,* this very moment, is creative, Creativeness renewing Itself *every moment.* Therefore there is no past, no future, except in the mind. When this is understood there is no memory of right or wrong, no divisions, no nationality, no different creeds, nothing to hinder the Living Present which is the only Real, and the only Real is Love and Wisdom. It is God the Father of All. The Yoga of the Christ is above all other Yoga because it is *all-inclusive, it is everything, it is All* and exists NOW, ONLY NOW!

God exists in His completeness NOW! NOW! *and He alone is!*

When you realise this, there can be no high, no low, no good, no bad, in Reality. It is in man's mind that these exist and this is man's conditioning. When you know the self, the mind with its images, its beliefs, its ideas, its divisions, its yesterdays, its tomorrows, and all the illusions it creates, when this is seen freely without condemnation, without judgment, being creations of the self, to get beyond them the mind must cease to fabricate, for the mind is the great illusion and the cause of the illusion. It does not know, and what it does know is not the Real, it is merely ideas of the Real, which it believes to be the Real. The idea of God is not God, the word "God" is not God, but God is Eternal and Ever-present in his completeness and He is the only One. This can be experienced only when the mind is quiet. When the mind sees that it can never know, it ceases to struggle; then only is the Real which is *now* ! not something in the future which exists only in the mind.

You must experience this for yourself, no one can do it for you, the way you must go alone without teacher, without guru, *alone* only can you enter the *Unknown:* there is no other way. This is what I experienced. It was this I saw for myself. It was the yoga of the Christ.

A teacher is a hindrance to the experiencing of the Unknown, because there will always be the teacher and the other, but when the mind is silent there is never the one and the other, there is never the experiencer and the experience, for the self has dissolved in that Eternal moment. My words are inadequate, my words can never reveal the Unknown. It can only be uncovered from within and not from without.

Truth cannot be used. The moment you approach Truth with the desire to use it in the world of action you lose It, then the Truth and you become separate. There is the you and the Truth, but when you see that this cannot be the Truth, only an idea of It, then Truth is. You cannot use Truth as if it were a shovel or a pickaxe, for then you become greater than the Truth and this is impossible. But if you can realise the Truth and allow It to operate without wanting to use It, then It brings a fundamental transformation in your life and your relationship, and its operation is wide, unlimited, extensive.

Immediately you try to use the Truth as an instrument it is not the Truth but mere mental action which will have within it memory, division, good, bad, and all the illusions of the mind, hate, jealousy, antagonism, which is merely a projection of the self.

But if you allow Truth to operate within you and through you without interference from the mind, then unknowingly, unconsciously, It has far-reaching effects beyond human conception. Then you will experience the liberating effect of Truth---the Unknown---God or whatever name you may call It. The Unknown has no name, the Unknown is unpredictable, so you must understand that the mind cannot use It. But if the mind is quiet the Truth will operate and Its operation is extensive, wide, unlimited, and herein lies freedom and supreme happiness and the power and glory of the ever-present Infinite Life.

"Verily I say unto you, whosoever shall not receive the Kingdom of God as a little child shall in no wise enter therein." Luke 18:17.

CHAPTER VI

We were both in a state of true meditation. How long it lasted I did not know. When I returned to the world of time I felt rejuvenated. I must have looked many years younger, for my friend remarked: "What a remarkable transformation, you look many years younger," and I felt it. My body felt light, my mind alert and clear; it was a better instrument now through which Reality could function, for Reality created us for that purpose. I knew that everything would be well. I no longer relied upon my past experiences or memory as a guide. In fact I had no guide outside myself and my friend said these very words to me then: "My son, the only guide is the Unknown, the Uncreated. My experience, though perhaps much more than yours, is no longer a guide to you. Only my companionship now can give you what your heart desires. But your guidance comes from within.

"We will in future discuss, impersonally together, the problems that are not yet clear and, through the Love and Wisdom of God who is the very Livingness in both of us, the way is revealed. I of myself am nothing; it is the Livingness of God within us both that does the work. The Master's words were: 'I of mine own self am nothing, it is the Father who ever remains in me, He does the work.' So it is with us. God alone lives; therefore, when we understand that which is hindering the Livingness, it will no longer be a hindrance."

We had been in the front hall since early morning and now it was lunch-time. I said: "I feel that I have had so much food, may I have just a glass of milk again for my lunch?" So we both had milk for our lunch.

We discussed many things about my work in the world and the countries to which I would travel. Since then I have been in America, Canada, England, Scotland, Australia, New Zealand, South Africa, China, Japan and through the Middle East. My healing work has been phenomenal and for this I know I am not responsible, I of myself being nothing. This I learned in no uncertain manner. So

Chapter VI

I went as the Spirit directed.

After lunch I broached again the subject of climbing the peak Nyiblung Richung that stared us in the face, challenging us.

"Well," said my friend, "we will have to make arrangements. I can see you will never be satisfied till we have made the attempt. We will have to get good porters, of whom there are plenty in the district, good ones, as good as anywhere in the world. We will make the ascent in stages, for it is not going to be an easy task and it will take us at least ten days. We will have to arrange camps on the way up; the ropes and tackle for climbing I fortunately have here. If we are to do this climb we must do it now, otherwise the winter will be on us and then there is no hope, the snow will be too deep. There is also the danger of storms, and they are very fierce, lasting for days. If caught in one of these it is doubtful whether we would survive in the mountains and I could not think of risking your life after we have brought you here, mainly for your work and not for climbing," He looked at me inquiringly.

I said: "I appreciate that, and I am not going to jeopardise all the good that you have done for me."

"Well," he said, "if we cannot get past the mushroom top we will agree to give up the task of climbing farther."

"Agreed!"

Arrangements were set in operation at once. The memory of the excited anticipation I had before climbing in the Southern Alps, and the difficult rock climbing in Scotland, was returning.

Climbing was in my blood, something within me always moved towards a challenger; but I also reminded myself that I was not to take risks as I did in the past. I knew I had been reckless in my younger days in doing dare-devil things which I need not mention here.

The party, when ready, consisted of twenty experienced porters, my friend, and myself, and so we started off. I remember that morning well; the sun had not yet risen. It was because the first part of the journey of five miles to the bottom of the glacier would be comparatively easy that we started before sunrise.

We reached the bottom of the glacier about 7 a.m. Then my friend put in hand the organising of our first camp on the spur on the right side of the glacier.

"This glacier,' he explained, "is fifteen miles long. We will make our first camp at the snow-line, the bulk of the stores that we need will be placed there, and when we reach there we will plan further."

So off we went again and it was not long before we had passed the wood-line, and we were now in the open. The wind was blowing fiercely and it hindered us. We skirted the glacier because of the danger of the crevasses and we had not the means of bridging them. This river of ice was particularly beautiful in its deep blue and white. I could see that some crevasses were at least twenty feet wide. To fall down one of these would be fatal.

We were making good time in spite of the high wind. The rock work was easy, until we reached some ice which had embedded itself into the rock for years---it was like glass and very slippery. We had special ice boots; mine fitted me perfectly and were extremely comfortable. My friend's feet and mine were of much the same size and I had chosen a pair which had done some work before. I softened them with yak butter and they felt safe around the ankles; they were easy on the feet and fitted like a glove. That is what you need in climbing, a well-fitting boot around the ankle, and then your feet feel safe as you grapple with the ice.

Chapter VI

My friend went ahead, for he was expert in cutting steps in the ice. I had climbed with many climbers before, but I never saw such an expert as my friend, and I am certain I will not find another with such judgment.

We rested the first day half-way; it was fair going. The porters came after us with the loads, and we bivouacked in a sheltered spot between two great rocks. At the side of the glacier we lit our spirit lamps and had some hot coffee, meat barley bread, butter and cheese. I felt good for I was hungry, and the air was crisp and fresh. The spot my friend chose was also sheltered from avalanches. We chattered for a while. I wanted him to talk to me on prayer, but he said: "You had better get some sleep, that's the best prayer now, so that you will be fresh for the morning. We will start as soon as there is sufficient light."

So I left the subject of prayer for a more convenient time, but I said: "Although we are climbing, it is not necessary to abandon our work completely."

"No, I have no intention of doing that, but let us do it when the time is more appropriate."

We got into our sleeping bags, gloves and balaclava headgear, and were soon sound asleep. I did not awaken till my friend tugged at my balaclava, and when I opened my eyes the rays of the sun were just showing themselves.

"There will be enough light by the time we have breakfasted," he said. So I put on my boots and jacket; we had breakfast in half an hour, and then we were off again.

All went well for about an hour, when we came to a dead stop. We came upon a perpendicular precipice of ice and rock welded together. I could not see any way out of the difficulty. My friend said: "There is only one way now unless we go down to where we started this morning, and go round to the other side of this precipice, but that means a day wasted. The only way is to climb the precipice. If that jutting piece of rock will hold we can do it; if we can throw a rope over it, it will be easy. When I get up I will pull you up, and we will do the same with two porters, and then they will manage the rest, and the stores as well."

Everything worked as planned. The rock held tight, and my friend got up above the solid wall of rock and ice, I got up afterwards, and we got all our stores and porters up safely.

When we reached the top of the glacier our leading porter said that if we made camp under the shelf of that spur on the right it would be half-way. We could also make another camp farther up. So we crossed over to the spur on the right. We were now cutting footholds in the hard ice-like snow, hardened by centuries of wind and snows.

Eventually we got over on the spur on the right and we made camp. We were now within 6,000 feet of the top. This was the third day of our hazardous journey.

My friend said: "We must reach the top within another three day, otherwise it will be too lake, for the winds blow here at hurricane speed and there is no hope after those winds have begun."

So, our camp established, we started our real climbing the next day. We were now using our ropes all the time, four of us, two porters, my friend and I being roped together. Eight other porters came on behind. They were expert climbers and I could see that their rope work was magnificent. They carried the stores necessary for our next camp; the remainder we had left behind at the camp below.

My friend went first, then one of the porters, called Namza, then myself, and lastly the other porter called Sipaho, meaning "evil averted". Namza meant "cover".

My friend's work with the ice-axe was superb; he cut each step with two strokes of his axe, and we made steady progress till we reached the mushroom top. My friend said: "I will investigate and see if there is a way up."

But I said: "I don't want you to go alone, I will come with you."

"No," he replied, "I am better alone, nothing will happen. Where is your faith you talked about the other night---has it been blown away with the wind?"

I pulled myself up with a round turn, for I had a lot of conditioning still to get rid of.

My friend went off alone. He was away for about an hour and we were getting anxious. An avalanche was in full force rumbling down the mountainside while he was out of sight. He had cut steps for himself in the snow and ice so quickly that he was out of sight in a few minutes.

I was glad when he returned. I said: "I have not yet got that faith that moves mountains. Yet it was growing, and this was a wonderful test." He looked at me but did not answer at the moment, and then a little later he said: "There is only one way that I can see, and that is to climb up that rock-face and then cross over on the top of this snow-covered cone to that spur that goes on the top. If the snow holds we can do it, but if the snow fails us, well, we will have to slide down a hundred feet on to that ledge. I think it is deep soft snow.

That is a chance we must take. But I think we can cross over the face of this cone all right. Do you feel you want to go on?"

I looked straight into his eyes and replied: "You do not think I would turn back now?" He smiled a smile of satisfaction and replied: "I knew you would say that."

We got all roped together again and did some very dangerous ice- and rock-work. We reached out on to the side of the cone that was defying us.

The snow held fast and we reached the spur. My friend said it would be more difficult to come back adding: "I think we will make our next camp here. This is the only way, I am sure; no one had found it up to now, probably could not get round that steep rock covered with ice."

"I don't know how you held on," I said. "I don't think there is another man in the world who would tackle that rock-face."

"The difficulty was to cut ice steps while clinging on to the rock-face," he modestly explained; and when I said: "It looked like you had suckers holding you on," we all laughed heartily, which was a relief from the tension of the last few hours.

We got on to the spur and when the others came we made camp for the night. We were now about 2,000 feet from the top and we felt sure of victory. Next day we rested so that we would be fresh for the final assault the following day.

Then on the final day we started at sunrise and reached the top at about noon.

The whole range of the Nyenchentangla peaks could be seen, and way down in the valley on the other side we could see a great lake about fifty miles long and about thirty miles wide. The mountain ran down right into the lake, which itself was over 15,000 feet above sea level. The name of the lake was Nam Tso or Tengri Nor. I counted thirty rivers running into this lake. Two of these rivers were very large ones called, respectively, Ngang Chu and Tri Chu. To the left lay unexplored country. Not a living soul seemed to be living there; but to the right, down on the side of the lake, there were a few houses. We could just pick them out, each house looking like the head of a pin, thousands of feet below us.

This was Tibet in the raw. My friend said that for centuries people were born there, lived there and died there, and probably not one of them had ever seen the outside of that valley. I remarked that I did not think they would have any desire to do so, it was all so beautiful.

"Yes," he replied, "it is a land that is strange all right, but the outside world to them would be even stranger."

We had accomplished what we had set out to do; it was a thrilling experience, a never- to-be forgotten experience. We were the only known people in the world to climb Nyiblung Richung!

We were all happy, and a sense of satisfaction swelled the heart. We had accomplished what we set out to do; it was a good omen and I knew it, and my friend said the same. That afternoon we started on our way down and reached the camp as the sun was setting. Words cannot reveal the beauty of that sight.

The coming down was easier than we had anticipated. We arrived back in Zamsar just ten days from the day we had left it. I would not have missed that experience; it was, as it were, part of my training. Difficulties melted away as we came upon them, and so it has been ever since. Difficulties have dissolved in a most miraculous manner.

God does the work when you do not try to use God like a tool, for your own use, but, when you allow Truth-God to operate, that operation is extensive, wide, unlimited, complete. Herein lies the secret of the Christ Yoga. God does the work. That is true faith and I found it to be true while climbing Nyiblung Richung.

The evening we arrived back, the whole town (if you could call it a town) was out to meet us and welcome us home, also to hear the good news. Did we make it? Nearly everyone had a relative in the party. There was great rejoicing, the news spread that night from one end of Zamsar to the other, and everyone gathered in the hall in the middle of town to celebrate. Everyone brought food and lots of barley beer, the national drink called *chang,* and lots of *tsampa,* a form of Tibetan bread. Eggs were passed round, not eggs for eating but as a ceremonial gift. Some of these eggs were a year or more old! The town sprang into a state of harmonious happiness overnight.

We, my friend and I, first went to my friend's sanctuary. We had not had a bath for ten days, though it is not the longest time I have had to go without a bath.

We got into the swimming pool of running water. The water was nice and warm and we washed ourselves at the out-flowing end. We got into fresh clothes and went down to the hall.

My friend said: "We must partake of some of the food that has been provided by the people for us at the hall." So we ate with relish. To my surprise, there was roast chicken and roast potatoes--- my favourite meal. It was good.

My friend, speaking in Tibetan, explained in detail how we reached the top of the previously unconquerable mountain. You could have heard a pin drop, everyone, even the youngest, was deeply interested in the climbing of Nyiblung Richung. Besides, my friend had a wonderful voice, you could not help listening to it, it fascinated you as he spoke.

Chapter VI

The Tibetan women are equal in every respect to the men, and many of them are magnificent climbers. They also plough and dig, carry water and cut wood. In the house and out of the house they are every bit as good as the men, and as traders they are far ahead of them.

All, young and old, had their fill of barley beer (*chang*). The Tibetans are naturally a happy lot of people; seldom do you see any quarrels, and the more *chang* they drank the happier they got.

Morals among the peasant folk are pretty loose, but no one takes any notice of that, and on this night there seemed no restraint. The Tibetans are passionately fond of children, and no one thinks anything of it if a girl has a child before she is married. It is seldom you see a woman after a certain age without a child, whether she is married or not, and a happier lot of people it would be hard to find anywhere else in the world.

The conditions of living are harsh in the winter, most of the time the temperature being below zero. But people are accustomed to these conditions; they know nothing else, and they take it all to be the natural thing.

My friend was the King of Zamsar. I could see that he was adored by everyone, young and old. His wisdom, love and understanding were the secret. I never heard a word of criticism from him, neither did he condemn. He was indeed the essence of Truth. With his mind freed from conditioning, Truth operated without hindrance or limitation.

It was not until the early hours of the morning that we turned in, and even then I did not feel tired, but I slept like a log, being completely satisfied.

When I awoke the sun was up. I looked over at Nyiblung

Richung, no longer with yearning but with a feeling of satisfaction, and I said to my friend: "It is a grand feeling I have this morning."

"Yes," he replied, "but we must get on with our work now."

I said to him: "I asked on the mountain about prayer, and I would be grateful if you would clarify the subject of prayer for me."

He said: "What does prayer mean to you?"

"Well, I generally pray when I want something or I am in trouble or I am sick; sometimes I give thanks,"

"Yes," he said, "when you pray you are mostly in a state of uncertainty, are you not? In a state of contradiction or when you are unhappy or when you are confused?"

"Yes, one seldom prays when one is happy and content."

"Then," he said, "prayer must bring some satisfaction, otherwise people would have given up prayer long ago. When you ask you receive, and you receive according to your belief; that is the natural outcome of prayer, is it not? Jesus said, 'Believe you have received it and you will have.' This is a truth.

"But when you pray you are seeking satisfaction in one form or another, and to a mind that is seeking gratification at whatever level, high or low, there is a certain amount of gratification according to your faith which is mostly blind faith. But there is a greater thing than prayer and we can discover it when we understand the ways of prayer.

"Now, what do you do when you pray? Don't you repeat certain words, take up certain postures and so forth, now you are looking for an answer. In this looking for an answer the mind is quietened somewhat, and in that quiet state you feel satisfied, and only in a quiet state is the mind capable of receiving an answer. But this does not help you, the petitioner, to understand yourself and it is only in understanding oneself that it is possible to get beyond this state of demanding, seeking, striving for a result."

"In prayer," he added, "you always have the outstretched hand waiting, hoping, and with hope there is a state of hopelessness. You are striving to lose one and gain the other. But you can see that prayer can never release the mind from creating the very conditions that make you pray. So there is always a state of uncertainty, and it is this state of uncertainty that demands prayer. Therefore the solution is to free the mind from manufacturing its own problems, is it not?

"Now prayer depends upon the petitioner. When one asks for something there is an unconscious experience of centuries, and according to the mental state of the petitioner he receives accordingly. As Jesus said: 'Believe ye have received and ye shall have.'

"But is the mind not all the time living in opposites, having and not having, health and ill-health, success and failure, good and evil, and so on? It is only when you understand the total process of the mind that you can go beyond, and this is much more important than prayer.

"Prayer has no solution for the petitioner, nor is prayer a solution to the petition! You may get what you wanted but that does not prevent the mind from manufacturing again the very thing that you pray for release from. So it is not the finding of a superficial answer to your prayer but understanding of the whole process of the mind that creates the problem from which you want release.

"The world has been praying for peace for centuries, but peace is just as far away. Why pray for peace if you do not understand the cause of war? Why pray for success if you do not understand the cause of failure? Why pray for health if you do not understand the cause of ill- health? Why pray for joy if you do not understand the cause of sorrow?"

"You do not pray when you are joyous, when you have no problems. You pray only when you are in conflict, when you have difficulties you cannot solve.

"What is essential is to understand the whole process of the mind---the self which is the cause of the problem. Then the mind no longer chatters nor has to be made quiet, but becomes quiet through right meditation, as I have already explained. In that quietness there is the Real, and with Reality there is no problem. The self alone makes the problem which the self prays about. The solution is understanding the cause of the problem and this is you---the self---and, when the self is understood to be what it is, having no existence in Reality, it dissolves away and so does the problem. Then Reality which you do not create but is Creativeness itself comes into Being immediately. *That is true prayer.* It is Being. The effectiveness, the extensiveness, the unlimited state of 'Being' has to be experienced to be realised."

I was in a silence that was not created, a silence that comes through understanding the ways of the self and what the self is. In this deep silence my mind had ceased to "chatter" as he called it, and Reality was. At that moment I knew that Reality had no problem. At that moment the problem dissolved itself into its native nothingness. *For Reality was all there is and, Being Creative, it cannot be created. What was manufactured was the problem that the mind itself manufactured and I knew the mind could not solve it. But the moment the mind---the me---saw this, it no longer chattered, the problem was no more.* This was the revealing of self- knowledge, and without self-knowledge there is no solution. This was true prayer. It was true meditation in which Reality operated, and this operation is wide and unlimited. *God occupied His own House completely.*

CHAPTER VII

I was beginning to understand the "Yoga of the Christ". But this was merely a name and in a name there is nothing. I could understand that now, though I always wanted a name for this book that I would eventually write. I knew that most people were attracted by a name, by a title, position, rank, ideas and all that the stupid mind feeds on. The mind can feed only on what it itself is made of, and that is merely ideas, words, beliefs and so on; and when the mind does not see its own stupidity, it keeps on manufacturing problems that agitate it, so it keeps chattering till such time as it begins to understand itself as the cause of the problem, it begins to understand itself and its movements.

Immature minds are always manufacturing problems, and they try to solve them on their own level. But this only creates more problems, and thus there is an endless chain of cause and effect that never ceases. This will end only when the mind begins to see how it itself is the cause of this state of affairs.

Politicians, economists, dogmatists and all other -ismatists are merely the product of an immature mind, and those imitators who follow are made up of the same material as their leaders.

It is not until we begin to think for ourselves that we wake up out of this hypnotic state. All the words in the world, all the books in the world, cannot help, they only hinder. They merely feed the conditioned mind with that which it seeks to confirm its conditioning. Therefore such a mind can never be creative.

Now, you who read this book may want to know how you may achieve Creativeness. In reading this book you may think that I am showing you how to become Creative, but I am not. You may think that by practising a technique you can become creative. Well, let me tell you, that that is impossible.

Chapter VII

Do you think that by practising eight hours a day on your musical instrument you can be creative? Writing books, composing music, writing poetry, making speeches, giving addresses, does not bring Creativeness. You may be a perfect speaker, a fluent writer, a good painter, but if the me is still present there can be no creativeness. Is it not the me---the self--- that stands in the way which is beyond the mind, which alone is creative? Unless the self is absent there can be no Creativeness.

When the self is present there is always conflict, is there not? That is easy to see, all you have to do is to look into your own mind. There can never be creativeness as long as there is conflict. Does not conflict prevent creative action? As long as the mind is caught between opposites there must be conflict which excludes creativeness. Only when the mind is quiet can there be a creative state. Creativeness is not created. Creativeness is; and can only come into operation when the mind understands itself and its way, its desire to express itself, striving for attainment which brings about contradiction. The Christ-Spirit of God in man is alone creative, and this you do not create.

It is only when the mind is entirely silent, free from its own demands, that there is a possibility of Creativeness. To most people Creativeness is self-expression which gives one a sense of importance, the feeling of being somebody. This feeds on the self which is vanity and ignorance and destroys the state of Creativeness.

Creativeness is from moment to moment, when the self is absent, when all opposites are silent. As long as the self is seeking to be creative, Creativeness can never be. Only when the self comes to an end does Creativeness come into being. I of *myself am nothing,* It is the Father alone who is Creative, when He alone does the work, that is true Creativeness.

Those words, though not the exact words as printed in the Bible by human hands as being the saying of Jesus, still convey the meaning I want to give, not that the word or the meaning of the word can convey Creativeness, only in the absence of the self can Creativeness operate and that operation is wide and unlimited, without opposition or conflict.

* * * * * * * *

If I were concerned whether this book would be accepted or not, it would never have been written. The self would be in the way. But, when the self knows itself, things are seen as they are, and there is no longer that desire to escape from them.

If the reader merely reacts because of his pet ideas or beliefs, if he accepts or rejects, he is not reading, he is merely reacting to what his mind is made up of. Then what he gets will be of little value. But if he or she reads in the deeper sense as a means of understanding the self and how the mind is conditioned, then transformation comes. Transformation is not made up in the mind; it comes as a result of the dissolving of that which is hindering the operation of the Real. Only by seeing things as they really are does the mind cease to chatter, and in the quietness that follows *the Real is.*

We worked steadily on each day. Our discussions were revealing in the true sense of the word, and it was this revealing that was necessary for me. For I had been caught up in the various systems of Yoga which were mental, and though I could do many wonderful things I came to understand how they were a hindrance to the freedom of the Christ, which is the love and wisdom of God.

Most books written about Truth---new thought, or whatever name they give it---are, if you observe, merely mental. What I mean by "mental" is that it is all made up in the mind and what the mind makes up is not Truth, but merely an idea of Truth. The mind can do wonderful things through concentration and Yoga exercises, yet you will see, if you look, that it is merely the self that is at work. But the Christ Yoga is only possible when the self--the mind---is quiet.

My friend would begin with these words: "Only by understanding what the mind is made up of, can the Real which is beyond the mind to be revealed. But if there is the self and the Other, the Truth cannot be, the self is always in front. Then Truth becomes a means to an end. But Truth is not a means and has no beginning or ending. Therefore what you have is but a projection of the self."

Then we would begin our discussion remembering that fact.

A question I asked once was: "How can we know anything if thought ceases?" This is a question you, too, may be asking at this moment, and it is not the first time I have been asked the very same question.

"If I ask you that question you respond to the challenge, you begin to think!" My friend said: "So your thinking is a response to a challenge, but that response is always the result of the past, because the mind is made up of what is past, it does not know the New."

"Yes," I said, "I can understand that."

"Then I may ask you a question in a few minutes' time and that will be another challenge. You begin to think again."

"Yes, that is true."

"Now," he asked, "what is this response? The challenge may be always new but your response, your answer, comes from memory, from experience, then the response is always old, is it not?"

"Now," he continued, "I will ask: do you believe in God? There may be an immediate response but it is a response through your conditioning. You may say 'No' because you do not believe in God, that is because your mind is conditioned by the belief that there is no God, or you may say 'Yes' also because you believe there is a God. But you merely believe or disbelieve because your memory tells you so.

"Your memory is the result of experience, and experience is knowledge, and knowledge is of the past. But you can never know God through knowledge or experience. So thinking is the response to the background of the past. It is response at different levels, individual and collective, according to your background, race, creed, beliefs, knowledge and customs, conscious and unconscious, therefore your thinking can never be new. What your mind accepts now, is old the moment afterwards. You can think only of the moment that is past, which is memory; you can know the present only when the mind is still, you can't think about it. If you do it is past.

"In that living moment you are aware but you cannot think because you do not know what it is, the self has disappeared. Now that moment that is past is memory, but the living moment is still the living moment in the present. You want to think about that experience, so now there is you and the experience, but the experience is past, it is not the living moment that is always present moment to moment in which there is no you, there is just the Living Presence, the Real Eternity. But you don't know what it is: when it is past you try to recapture it but you can't, it is a memory because it is past, you are now thinking of the past, the known, and the known is always the past. But the ever-present moment is always New, that is why you can't think about It, It is always beyond the mind. It is, when the mind is quiet, there is only experience. But now the mind is active and there is you and the experience, but that is the past, is it not? It is most essential that you understand this, otherwise you can never know the Yoga of the Christ.

"You see now that thinking can never renew itself. It is always the old, and what it renews is the old, the old being your conditioning, your tradition, your race, your experiences, your beliefs, therefore thought can know only its own projection, thought can recognise only what it has already experienced.

"Thought, then, is merely recognition. It can never know anything beyond itself. Thought, you can see now, is merely symbols, words, images, experiences, and without these there is no thought. Therefore thought can never be creative because it know only what is past, it can never think on that which it does not know. It cannot experience that which is beyond it, because it can recognise only the old and never the new. What you experience becomes memory and your thought is the product of memory."

"Yes," I said, "now that you have put it so plainly before me I can understand that thought is limited to what is in the mind. So it can never know the new, only the old. Thought can never know that which is beyond mind; it can project only what is in the mind and that is memory."

"There is nothing abstract about it," he continued, "for if you look carefully you will see as long as the 'I' which is a mental recognition of itself, which is made up of memories and is experiencing these memories in words, images and symbols, while thought is only experiencing the past, it can never discover the new. Therefore it can never experience God or Reality which is the Unknown, which is the Unimaginable, the Uncreated, the Unformulated, which has not symbol, no word.

"The word 'God' is not God, neither is God an image; God is not a thought, otherwise you would know what He was, but you can see that is impossible because God is beyond mind. The mind can only function within the field of the known; it cannot function beyond it."

"I can see that plainly now," I said, "I can see clearly that immediately I think about the Unknown the mind becomes active, it is always seeking to bring the Unknown into the field of the known, and that is obviously impossible. For the Unknown can never be the known; the Hermit of Ling-Shi-La showed me that in no uncertain manner."

"Yes," he said, "it is only possible for the Unknown to be, when thought ceases. So there is no question of the 'I' ever experiencing the Unknown. The 'I', the mind---the self---are one and the same, and the self is merely a bundle of ideas, images, words, symbols, which is memory, and can recognise only its own projection.

"When the mind says that it is certain that it has experienced the Unknown, it is not the Unknown it has experienced but a projection of itself, which is not the Unknown but which it believes to be the Unknown. But when the mind sees that it assumes its own projection to be the Unknown it becomes quiet, it is no longer agitated by its seeking, and in the silence that follows the *Unknown* is; then only does the Unknown operate without hindrance and its operation is unlimited. Thought is limited to the past, to memory, but the Unknown is always now. It is always new, moment to moment without limitation."

He paused and then continued: "When you think you are experiencing the Unknown you are merely expressing a new sensation of the mind. But sensation or idea is not the Unknown. The Unknown can never be recognised. *The Unknown is.* It is not created, what you create is merely an idea of the Unknown, a projection of the mind---the self. You cannot create the Unknown. You know that now, don't you?"

"Yes," I said, "that is quite clear."

"For the Unknown to be," he explained, "you must understand

the whole process of thinking, that is the working of the mind which is the self, and when the self sees it is merely a bundle of memories, experiences, ideas, images, symbols, it no longer tries to experience the Unknown and becomes quiet. Only when the mind is still, utterly still (not made still) in that stillness, that tranquillity, the *Real is.*"

I was glad of this revealing discussion in detail which I was told my friend would give me; and I know it will help you also to realise that the known can never be the Unknown; you will see that thinking can be only the expression of the past.

But NOW, the ever-present NOW, is Reality, this very moment when thinking has come to an end. Living moment to moment, time disappears; this you can experience only when you are not thinking, free from the past or the future which is in the mind---the past is memory and the future a hope which is a projection of the past, because you only think of the future in terms of the past. *Pure thinking comes through Inspiration which is the expression of the now, moment to moment.*

Jesus said, in other words, "Take no heed for the future, sufficient unto the moment is the evil thereof."

On another occasion I asked this question: "In the light of our understanding, how do the words of the prophets, including those of Jesus, reveal the Truth?"

"Well, my son," he answered, "you know that words can never reveal the Truth. Jesus said, "It is the word that killeth," meaning the word hides the Truth. But we can reason towards the Truth, yet reason must cease before we enter the door of Silence which is the entrance of Truth.

"You see, my son, all the so-called holy words have been written by men that is the first thing to consider. The New Testament was written 150 years after Jesus was crucified, which was the method of murder at that time. Today in the West there are other ways of murdering people, the hangman's rope, the guillotine, the electric chair, the gun, the bomb and other devices.

"If someone murders another person you call him a murderer, don't you? Then you murder the murderer, but are you not a murderer too?"

"People today think that they are doing God a service by murdering others who do not believe in the way they do.

"Mass murder is taking place all over the world today as the result of this belief. To murder without consent you get the hangman's rope, but to murder by consent you get a medal. But it is murder just the same. You cannot deny that, can you? Now you also see that those who assume the representation of the Deity bless those sent out to murder, also bless the weapons manufactured for murdering. They assign to their God characteristics that you and I would not attribute to the most backward savage. If you read your Bible you will see that what I say is true, yet they call it a Holy Book.

"Now, some will say that times have changed, that man is more developed, but is he? He is more subtle, he kills more people than he did a hundred years ago, but it is done in a flash and the result is more devastating.

"Today we have guns and bombs instead of bows and arrows. We have bombs that will destroy thousands at a time, we have incendiary bombs that burn with agonising pain, causing more pain than an arrow could ever do, yet we are told that we are more developed. Yes, we have developed the means of killing more people, but it is still killing is it not? No matter how we murder people it is murder just the same, the end is the same; the weapons are more deadly and we say more humane, but are they more humane? And the cause of all this carnage is division in nationalities, in race, in religion, in beliefs and ideals. The idealist is the most dangerous person because to make his ideal work he must be ruthless; he kills all those who oppose him.

"People are killing each other today more for their ideals than for things. To protect their ideals they have to kill, so we see mass murder going on directed by those who go to church, and pray to a God of Love whom they claim to be their Father. What a travesty of the Truth! Spirituality is all-inclusive. If you love one and hate another you cannot be a loving person, therefore you cannot be spiritual, you live in contradiction.

"Jesus the Prophet said: 'Love your God and love your neighbour.' But the only way to love God is to love your neighbour, and why don't we love our neighbour? Simply because he has a different religion, a different nationality. Therefore one has to see what ideals are, what beliefs are, what nationalities are, what organised religion is. These things are the product of the immature minds, are they not? It is quite obvious to a man of sense.

"1 Kings, chapter 7, verse 21 indicates that there are two pillars set up by Solomon at the entrance of the Temple. On the right is the Pillar of Jakin and on the left is the pillar of Boaz. The Temple indicated here was a temple not made with hands, the Temple of the Living God, which God himself created. Life created the body and Life is God, for there can be no Life apart from Him who is Life. As the Prophet said, 'It is the Eternal speaking, I am the only One, there is none other beside Me,' and Jesus said, 'As the Father hath Life in Himself He grants the Son to have Life in himself.'"

"Now what do the words Jakin and Boaz signify? The English 'J' stands for the Oriental 'Y'. Jakin is therefore Yakin which means 'One'. This signifies the principle of unity as the foundation of all things.

"The Universal mathematical elements throughout the Universe are evolved from the One and resolve themselves back into One again. This mathematical element is not the living Life but the recognition of what the One Life gives rise to.

"Now to balance the mathematical element we need the vital element so then we have the pillar called 'Boaz' which means voice. Voice is the Living expression of the Creator, for Spirit alone has Voice. 'The word was in the beginning, that Word was with God and God was that Word.'

"The meaning is plain: to enter the Temple we must enter through these two pillars. It is symbolic of the Cosmos in the Temple of the Living God not made with hands.

"Jesus was referring to this temple when He said, 'Destroy this temple and I will raise it up in three days.' Those ignorant of the Truth thought he meant the synagogue but Jesus was referring to the Temple of the Living God, not a heap of stones which most people look on today as the Temple of God and is more important to them than the Temple not made with hands. *Their idea of God is more important than God Himself.*

"Dogma and creed is the narrow bigoted way that leads us into the building made with hands. But Jesus was showing the way into the inner Temple, the building not made with hands, where all the mysteries of Life will be unfolded to us in a regular order of succession as we begin to discern that which is not true---that which is false.

"The meaning is clear: the way cannot be through churches, gurus or priests, but through the unity of the one Life which is the Living Christ within. 'He who climbs in another way is a thief and a robber.'

"The opening up of these inner mysteries is not for mere gratification or curiosity, nor for material or spiritual gain as most people desire. It is for increasing of our Life-giving in Love and compassion, and this can only be done when the mind sees the stupidity of its own fabrications.

"The Living Christ beyond ideas is the Shepherd, the Life of the Father is the same as in the son. It is the Father alone who lives.

"The gate-keeper is the Father and everyone is known to Him, 'not a single one of these little ones can be lost.' They will know His voice and will not follow a stranger. They, knowing the Truth, will turn from him who preaches separation, so those who follow the stranger are the goats.

"Anyone who lives in separation is a stranger, is he not? But the Christ of God is the Livingness within every soul. When this is known it is possible to go in and out---meaning that when the Truth is revealed you can go out into the relative world and partake even there of all the good things that God has prepared for those who love Him, while still holding on to the Tree of Life which is man's salvation.

"Jesus again spoke in no uncertain terms when he said, 'Yes, it is about you, you hypocrites, indeed, that Isaiah spoke as it is written, "These people honour me with their lips, but their heart is far away from me, vain is their worship of me for the doctrine they teach is but human precept".' The text he was referring to was in Isaiah 29, verse 13, which reads, 'Since this people draw near Me with their mouth,' says the Eternal, 'honouring me with their lips, while their hears are far remote; since their religion is a mockery, a mere tradition learned by rote.'

"Jesus also says, "I have other sheep too, which do not belong to this fold, I must bring them also and they will listen to my voice (the voice of the Christ within), so it will be one flock and one shepherd,' meaning that all nations, all peoples of the world will eventually turn within, away from without, and will listen to the Spirit of God that is in each and everyone. Thus there will be one Life, one God, one shepherd, one flock (no separation).

"The Universal Life and the individual Life are one and same. There cannot be division. Only in the mind of man does this exist. This Life is the fulfilment of all our needs. Jesus says,

'I and the Father are one,' 'I of myself am nothing, the Spirit of the Father within me does the work.' This is the Christ Yoga. Yoga means united, all united in the One Spirit of God which is the Christ in man. Therefore the Christ Yoga is the unity of the Christ, that is the Spirit of God in each and every one.

"Only in understanding what the self is, and its ways can all the stupid action of man be dissolved. In the quiet of the mind is the inner Temple revealed; there, in that Silence that is not created, is Creative Understanding, Compassion and Love. Without these there can be no goodwill between man and man. Only by right means can right action come about. Wrong means will bring only emptiness and death. Peace and Love come from within, not from without. These things are not created by man; they come into being immediately man understands himself."

With this he ended his talk. It was a new phase showing that the Prophet's word were showing the way for man's salvation.

There followed a period of quiet.

It was I who broke the Silence. "Yes," I said, "we deliberately organise mass murder which creates more murderers. We are the creators of our own misery and degradation, corruption and destruction. When we are engaged in organised mass murder of others we bring into our own lives a host of other disasters and there is no end to it. We give preference to false values and disregard eternal values and the result, we say, is an act of God. But God's purpose is living, and not killing. There seems no end to this ever expanding desire to conquer, for possession, for power, to protect our ideologies. It is truly the blind that lead the blind into destruction."

And I quoted: "Truly, truly I tell you, we are speaking of what we do understand, we testify to what we have actually seen."

The he prayed as no one ever prayed before:

"O Divine Spirit, it has been revealed to us all that blinds us to Thy Presence. With Love alone we have discerned the false and now, Beloved, all fear, hatred and struggle have disappeared with the self.

"Now that we have seen man's inhumanity to man we will abide in Thee only and our actions will be Thy Will, O Beloved.

"Thy Presence alone is our happiness, in Thy Presence all inward poverty has dissolved away.

"In Thy Heart we love, O Divine Heart. "Thy Love, our Love, O Divine Love."

* * * * * * * *

His body and face appeared in a glorious light, the Love of God beyond man's conception. His words were pearls of great beauty strung on a garment of Love.

He was indeed a friend to the whole world.

CHAPTER VIII

When I got up the following morning I said to my friend: "I can seen that the prophets veiled their words so that only those who had reached a high spiritual state of understanding could read the hidden meaning."

"Yes," he agreed, "that has always been the way up to now. But now we have to speak in no uncertain terms without veiling our words. The time has come for the false to be shown up clearly, so that it can be understood and dissolved, thus ridding the world of the cause of its misery. In no circumstances must you veil your words or create ideas of the Truth; you must reveal the false; and when the false is clearly seen, then the Truth is, because it is not created.

"What we will do, form now onwards, is to go into more detail, so that you can understand the whole process of the mind of man which is the cause of all the trouble in the world today. We have to see the false clearly, more clearly than we have ever done."

I gathered from those few words that morning that there would be more intensive work to be done, and I found it to be so. I had to pay particular attention, otherwise I should have missed the points he was explaining.

My mind was clear and alert now, and I was aware of it; I could understand the deeper significance of what he said. Then he began:

"Today we will take memory as our subject because I want you thoroughly to understand the meaning of memory which is the cause of so much conflict.

"When you acquire technical knowledge, such as *facts* relating to a particular science, it is what we will call factual memory. Without factual memory you could not build a specific thing like a bridge or a railway engine, a motor-car or a house. This memory you will see is entirely different from memory of something unpleasant or pleasant that happened to you.

"Suppose someone said to you something unpleasant and another said something pleasant, you are immediately caught up in your reactions which become memory. The next time you meet the person who said the unpleasant thing, you meet him with that memory, is that not so? And the feeling you have is a reaction to the memory of yesterday, which you resent. You also meet the person who said the pleasant things with the memory of yesterday, but your reaction is quite different; nevertheless, the same function is memory, and this is what we will call psychological memory.

"We see now that we have factual memory or memory of facts, also we have psychological memory in which we have definite reactions, which is still memory. If you look into your mind you will see that you try to hold the pleasant memories and discard the unpleasant. A reaction is going on all the time, until you begin to realise that mind is memory or memory is mind, at whatever level, and has no existence in Reality.

"Now you begin to see that memory-mind is the result of the past, whether it is factual or psychological. Its foundation is the past which is a conditioned state. You see that, don't you?

"Now, let us look into this very carefully. We meet the new--- with the response of the old---memory; what is the result? Is not the new, conditioned by the past, the old? The challenge is always new but, in experiencing the new, the new is conditioned by the old. In those circumstances the new can never be thoroughly realised because you meet the new with the response of the old and this adds to the old. Therefore there can never be a realisation of the new in freedom because you experiencing is conditioned by the past, by the old.

"If you look into your mind now, you will see how you meet the new. If your mind is conditioned with religious prejudice, with nationalism with ideals, you cannot understand the new because the old stands as a barrier to understanding, which is continually strengthening the old in response to the new. All this, you will see, is incomplete experience. Therefore this incomplete experience will always rise to the surface to disturb you; that is why concentration on one idea means the suppression of all others, which are also incomplete.

"Now why does this incomplete experience trouble you? Because it is memory, and memory is an impression in the mind. But if you understand the whole truth of the matter you will see that Truth can never be a memory because Truth is beyond mind. Therefore Truth is always new, freed from memory. With this understanding only can you have complete experience, because there is true discernment, of what the mind is made up of without distortion.

"If your memory is used as a guide to the new, you will note that the new will be the old, will it not? When you have not fully understood the old-memory, you want to maintain it, do you not? In fact you cannot help but retain it. It is only when you see the Truth about something completely that you find that there is no memory in regard to it.

"Now, let us look at the ways we cultivate memory. You repeat mantrims, you read books, you have religious beliefs, ideals and all the rest of the junk with which you clutter up your mind. Now when you come to the new, what do you find? You meet it with the old! Now, memory has become more important than the new, is that not so?"

I did not answer; my tongue seemed incapable of forming any word. A transformation was taking place, I was seeing something I had not realised before, my understanding of the mind and its movements became clearer, when I realised that it was myself and I was the sole creator of the illusion.

"Now," he continued, "when we are young we look to the future and when we are old we live in the past! Why is this? Merely because we do not live now, in the present. In fact we cannot live in the present when we make the future more important; when we see this clearly, there is a complete understanding of yourself-myself, and to understand myself, what I am exactly now, does not need memory. Memory is a hindrance to the understanding of myself, Only when I know that memory is, does its significance dissolve away.

"You will note if you watch carefully that a new thought, a new feeling, comes only when the mind is not caught up in memory.

"If you had no memory, your possessions, your beliefs, your religion, your nationality would not be important. Therefore memory strengthens the self which is the cause of conflict, that is why you must understand memory and when you understand memory its significance fades away.

"But if you see that memory creates yesterday, today and tomorrow, that memory shapes today and tomorrow; you will see it is the past that is projected into the present and the future, because the living Present is not realised.

"How can you realise the Eternal, the Unknown, through the past, through memory? But this is what all so-called Truth students are trying to do. THEY ARE TRYING TO KNOW REALITY THROUGH MEMORY,

AND THAT IS WHY THEY ARE EVER-SEARCHING BUT NEVER-FINDING It is your work to show the falseness of this projection of the self, which is memory, and the assumption that this projection is the real when all the time it is memory.

"The Real can only be, when the *me,* which is memory, ceases to be. When you see that through memory you can never realise the Real, then you will understand this psychological memory that maintains the self which is a hindrance to the Real. When you see the truth of this the false falls away.

"Yes, memory makes life dull and empty for we live in conflict because of memory. You see now that psychological memory is a hindrance, while memory of facts is essential to our daily living; without it we could have no communication with one another."

"I can see now," I said, "that I have to understand what memory is, to see it for what it is. Then it is no longer a hindrance to the new. The new to be ever new, there must be no response through yesterday."

"Yes," he replied, "when this is understood, the Real---which is Wisdom---will operate in and around you.

"You talk about your spiritual counterpart, but surely, when you talk about your spiritual counterpart it is merely an idea of it! When you see this is false you are free from it, are you not? This is liberation, and in liberation the Real is. Do you understand?"

"Yes," I replied, "I do understand now."

With this he rose, gathered his robes and went away, leaving me alone to work it out for myself.

* * * * * * * *

My mind was giving up its old scars of memory. I could see that it was my self, caught up in the illusion of my importance. I was affected by what people said and did. Memories kept rising up before me and I could now understand the whole process; all those incomplete experiences were now being completed, because I realised that my self was the cause of the conflict, and the memory of these was dissolving and had no significance.

I was seeing them impersonally, without fear, resentment or condemnation, because they were the result of what I was myself.

When I saw what I was myself, at that moment, I was free. I, myself, was the cause. My reactions were the protection of my conditioning which could never be Reality. Reality had no reaction; only the self had reaction because I did not understand the self.

This self-revealing was freedom. I saw that memory, thought, the past, the future, was myself and I was not separate from it. When I saw that I was not separate from memory, thought, reaction, these being my own creations, the result of memory, and had no Reality in them, I lost all fear, hate, vanity, jealousy, and I no longer judged or condemned. Now I knew what the Master meant when he said: "Condemn not lest ye be condemned." Then all this conditioning-thought-memory fell away. I saw it was not real, it was the self bound up in its own creations.

I wonder if you can now at this moment feel the freedom that comes through understanding the self. In this way transformation takes place and Reality operates without limit, and great is Its operation, but you can experience It only moment to moment for It is the Living Present, and is without any conditioning whatsoever. Then, to live in the present is the Yoga of the Christ.

It was only when the gong boomed for lunch that I came back into this world of time and knowing what time was; there was a sense of Eternity that was very real to me now.

My friend had been down to the town and I met him in the hall. He put his arm around my shoulders and said: "Each time I look into your face I see the transformation."

And he added: "I have some news for you. Norbu and her family have come back and are anxious to meet you again. Norbu is very beautiful; I think you have awakened in her a love that is of the heart and must be understood. I saw it in her eyes when she spoke of you today."

He paused. Then: "I want to warn you because you have magnetic power, otherwise you could not be the healer that you are. Now! Norbu has asked me if she could come and serve in the house and do your washing and generally help in your comforts. I could not refuse because we never refuse the gift of service, for through unconditioned service love comes into being."

I replied: "I understand what you mean completely; I have experienced before the expression of love in service and what it means."

"Yes," he said, "true love is of the heart, not of the mind. Love is not a thought, it is much deeper than that and more profound. Without Love, Life has no meaning. That is the sorrowful part of most people's existence; they grow old while not yet mature. They read and talk about love but have never known the real fragrance of Life, and therefore the warmth of the heart that enriches Life is sadly missing. Without the quality of Love, do what we will, we can never solve any problems.

"The struggle to be chaste in thought is to be unchaste because in this there is *no* Love. To *truly Love* is to be chaste, pure, incorruptible. To solve the problem through logic is absurd; to approach it through religion is childish and stupid. To adjust it through glandular action or surround it with taboos shows a lack of understanding of our relationship with one another. To be aware of our thought-feeling-reaction in our relationship is a self-revealing process and in this revealing process is the Real.

"Only through thoroughly understanding ourselves can we reach that which is beyond the self. We do not create Love, Love comes into being when the self has died in its own revealing process."

* * * * * * *

The more I saw my friend and listened to his words, the more I realised his great wisdom and understanding. To be with him even without uttering a word was to experience that which was beyond the self, beyond mind, what was in the mind could be put into words, but that which was beyond mind could not be put into words. It could only be experienced.

CHAPTER IX

About tea-time Norbu arrived. In her hair she wore a chinese poppy which grew wild in the valley. She was truly a picture of great rarity. There was not the slightest sign of shyness about her. I was amazed at the natural way she spoke to us; there was a freedom that I had never experienced with the opposite sex before, and I knew how she acquired it. I could see my friend had done a lot in that direction.

When I looked into her wide-open blue eyes which looked into mine with a fearless frankness I could see that her mind was clear of all illusion. There was no feeling of uneasiness in our relationship. She spoke in excellent English with a fascinating accent, and as she spoke her face lit up with a charming smile showing a set of flawless teeth through her well-formed mouth. I was struck with her personality which was enhanced by her beauty and freedom.

I said to her: "You are a very lovely girl, Norbu." But what I said did not disturb her in the least one way or another.

The she said: "May I ask your permission to come and be of help to you?"

"It will be very nice to have you about the house, Norbu," I said, "but I have a lot of work to do and I am sorry I can't spend all the time I would like to with you."

"Since I was a girl of twelve years old I have been taught by my Master," looking at my friend with a look of appreciation and gratitude.

"Yes," I said, "I owe a very great deal to him too, more than I can say in words. One thing, I learned to know the self, that stupid self, that bubble has burst all right," and we laughed heartily, knowing well how that was done.

99

Chapter IX

There was no strain in our relationship and I knew now what true relationship meant, for without love there would be no relationship.

Norbu was the most efficient girl I have ever seen in any home. She decorated the table every day with wild flowers from the valley. She looked after our needs in every way and cooked delicious dishes out of the limited materials she had at hand. She was never idle for a moment. My clothes were seen to, sock, shirts, etc. Everything that could be done for our comfort was done by her.

One day I said: "Norbu, you are spoiling me utterly. I will never be content with anyone else after all you are doing for me." He face lit up with joy when I said this, and she looked even more beautiful than ever. In fact, during the time I was there she was becoming more beautiful every day and I told her so.

In the evening when we were not working she played her guitar and sang in her lovely soft soprano voice Indian and Tibetan lyrics.

When I showed a friend of mine in Hollywood (he was a film producer) her picture and told him about her, he wanted to get her to Hollywood to make a picture he had in mind about the Himalayas, around the story I had told him, but I said that was impossible.

One evening, when we were talking about the outside world, I said to Norbu: "The world I come from is full of sophisticated and insincere people. Most people are nice to your face but talk beyond your back. In fact, most people in my world are hypocritical, even the best of them are conditioned in one way or another.

"Yes, Norbu, they will love you at a distance because to them you would be a symbol, an ideal. But when you come among them they would be spiteful and jealous. The symbol of you would die a sudden death and they would seek another symbol into which they could escape. Their minds may be full of ideals but their hearts are empty, and it is what is in the heart that counts.

"Most people cling to an ideal of what they should be, but are afraid to see themselves as they really are, so their ideal is a wonderful escape but can never bring freedom. When they see themselves as they really are without criticism or condemnation or judgment, their false state will fall away and the Real which is not created will come into being. Few are they who can discern their thought-feeling-reaction and see themselves as they really are. They would rather hide behind an ideal than look at themselves, but only by doing so and understanding themselves is there freedom, beauty and love. For these are not created; they are ever-present and eternal and come into being only when the false falls away."

I knew then that there was no difference between man and woman as regards the Truth, man and woman were equal in every respect and could realise the truth according to the awareness of that which was hiding it and that was the self.

Far from being a disturbing influence Norbu was a treasure, and I gained wisdom from her actions. Her actions were the result of her unconscious thinking which was natural to her, having freed from the bondage of the self.

Norbu never sought to draw attention to herself but was always ready to serve without restraint. She was always ready to give of herself, yet never sought anything for herself. Yet she had everything because she was free. I could see that she did not live in opposites. As a life-companion it would be hard to find a more perfect one.

Her life was one of joy and happiness with us, and at times she would enter into our discussions with a wisdom and understanding which amazed me.

My friend said to me one day when we were alone: "Norbu is going to miss you more than you can realise when you leave here. You seem to creep into the heart of everyone you come in contact with, and I shall miss you more because of that also. Since your coming in the flesh into this land you have entered into the hearts of all you have come in contact with."

"Here," he said, "is a note from the Abbot of Ok, another from Geshi Rimpoche, and one from Tung La. They speak of you in terms of deep affection.

"Yes," I said, "but I also love every one of you and I will feel the parting more than anyone can know, for deep in my heart now is that sadness as I think of it. In fact I have often said to myself, why should I leave here where my real friends are? But I knew what your answer would be and therefore I never uttered a word?"

"Yes, my son, I know how you feel, but you have much work to do in your world, much as we love you to stay with us because of our love for you, but that cannot be."

At that moment I felt so unworthy of the trust put in me. I also felt that I was a mere speck on the horizon. Then my friend spoke again, for he must have read my thoughts:

"Remember," he said, "that the self is nothing, it is the Spirit that does the real work. The self can do nothing, it is more often a hindrance. When this is realised it no longer gets in the way."

I felt an immediate relief. I was no longer responsible. There was a greater power at work, and the more I got rid of the self the greater would be that power. My fear left me, my feeling of unworthiness fell away, and again I was as I was when he stripped me of the self long ago.

Only when the self is in evidence is there fear. I knew that now, and he understood as he looked into my face.

The night Norbu came to us we sat up till nearly midnight listening to her experiences during her journey to Lhasa and back. At the end she said: "I am glad I am back for I seemed to loose all confidence when among the paraphernalia and religious plays."

"Yes, Norbu," said my friend, "there are two types of confidence. One who has mastered a technique has confidence in himself as a technician, and you will see that this type of confidence is merely superficial. But there is another type of confidence that comes from knowing oneself, both in the active or conscious and the latent or unconscious spheres of the mind. When the whole surface and hidden mental activities are known, there is a confidence that is not self-assertive or shrewd, not the confidence that comes from memory of achievement, but a confidence that comes from seeing things as they really are.

"When confidence is based upon the belief in personal salvation, aggrandisement or achievement, it is pregnant with fears. But when there is an understanding of what ritual is, when there is an understanding of relationship with people, with things, with ideas, that understanding frees you from all authority. Therefore there is not the master and the pupil, or the *guru* sitting on a platform and the *chela* sitting below. When this is understood it frees you from all sense of time and authority.

"Such confidence is pregnant with love and affection, and when you love someone there is neither high or low, for Love itself is its own Eternity.

"In this state of being there is inward tranquillity in which there is love, kindliness, generosity, mercy. That state of being is the very essence of beauty. Without that, merely to adorn oneself with robes and paraphernalia is emphasise the values of the senses which lead to the illusion of high and low, and this leads to conflict and separation.

"The confidence of the Christ or the Buddha lies in a swift pliability of mind, and this is not only for the privileged few. There is but one Life and that Life will operate in its fullness in anyone who is aware of that which is hindering It."

I could see now, how Norbu had gained that freedom that comes from understanding, that perfume of existence she was expressing at that moment

I said: "What a privilege to be near the fount of wisdom always, Norbu. I wish I could be also."

"You can, we would love to have you with us always." My friend looked at her and said just one word: "Norbu."

Then there was silence; we all had our thoughts. The whole atmosphere was filled with a harmonious feeling of love that was beyond the physical.

It was I who broke the silence: "There is no separation anywhere, Norbu. In spirit we are ever together like pearls strung on that unbreakable chain of Love that is everlasting."

Tears welled up in her eyes as she said: "I know. I became possessive for a moment but now it no longer exists, because there is no separation except in the mind, never in the heart."

My friend then spoke: "I think you had better lay the supper, Norbu, and afterwards we shall go to rest. It is almost midnight and I see you are getting tired."

Norbu then laid a dainty supper of cold roast chicken and potatoes steamed in butter, and we all enjoyed this midnight meal.

Chapter IX

Next morning there was a delightful atmosphere; everyone was joyful. The night's sleep had worked wonders. I could hear Norbu singing a happy Tibetan song. When I asked her what it was, she replied: "It is one I made up myself."

"Tell me what are the English words, Norbu," I asked. She laughed and went on getting the breakfast ready.

After breakfast my friend said to me: "We will go up the valley today; I would like to discuss some more details that would be beneficial to you in your work."

So we wandered up the valley and sat on a rock covered with rock grass. All around our feet were wild flowers, wild poppies, wild rhubarb flowers, and about us were rhododen- dron trees in full bloom. It was truly a lovely spot to listen to that great sage.

He began with these word in his wonderful voice: "I tell you truly 'In as much as you did it to one of these my brethren even to the least of them, you did it to me.' It is recorded that Jesus said these words and I want you to observe their true meaning in your daily living, for in this observation there is true happiness.

"This great truth is not realised because the mind of man is caught up in separation, in ideals, in beliefs, that separate man from man.

"The idea that God, man and the Universe are one does not reveal the Truth. In fact it is merely a mental image you have acquired into which you want to escape, and this blinds you to the Real. But if you discern that this is merely an idea you can go beyond and experience the Truth of It.

"If you look carefully you will see that your thought is the expression of your particular conditioning and there would be no thought if there were no conditioning. According to what you are, so

105

is your thought. If you are a Socialist you think that way; if you are a Capitalist you think that way. If you are a Protestant, a Hindu or a Catholic, your thinking will be according to your belief. All your accumulated knowledge or learning becomes memory and this conditions you, and through this conditioning your thoughts are formed.

"Now without understanding this conditioning which is you, whatever you think and act will be according to that background. You see that clearly, don't you? You have only to listen to others and you will become aware of their conditioning; thus you can see yourself. To bring about a radical change in oneself there must obviously be an understanding of how this conditioning has come about. When this is understood, then there is an understanding of the self and how the self has become involved. When this is seen impersonally without distortion, there is freedom and in that freedom is the Real which is not a condition of any kind.

"Now most people seek wisdom through books; they think they can understand Life by following a so-called expert who says he knows, but he who says he knows does not know. Some join philosophical societies or religious organisations and an endless search goes on. Surely understanding and wisdom cannot be found in this way, for this is merely imitation, and imitation is not understanding. Merely accepting an idea is not understanding.

"If you merely accept that which confirms your conditioning or close up when your opinions are contradicted, there can be no understanding. Some make an effort to understand, but this merely changes their ideas.

"Transformation comes when you begin to see from where your thinking arises. Then there is understanding of what the self is. The self is your conditioning, the self is the projection of your conditioning, is that not so?"

"Yes," I said, "I now realise that more clearly."

"Life is free from conditioning therefore Life is Creative. To be creative then you must understand the self which prevent Life's expression. Right thinking comes when we know ourselves, and to know ourselves we must be aware of our thought-feeling-reaction, which is but a response of our accumulated past and when you understand how this accumulation has come about there is freedom."

"It is now becoming more and more clear," I ventured to say.

"We must be aware of our ideas, beliefs, desires, fears, antagonisms, our complete thought-feeling-reaction must be discerned as it affects the present, otherwise we will be giving expression to our conditioning. That is also clear, is it not?" he asked, and went on: "If your thought is moulded into a pattern, your thought-feeling-reaction will be within that pattern, ye see that, don't you? Your thought shapes itself according to your background. When you understand this, there is a stillness that is not created. The mind becomes still without being forced, because the mind---the self---sees what it is, and therefore ceases to project itself. When, then, the self sees that it is the cause of its own conditioning and cannot be separate from it, it ceases to seek an escape. When things are seen as they really are there is an understanding of them, and in this understanding there is freedom and in freedom there is Reality. When the mind is no longer burdened you will experience this freedom.

"The mystery of the power of Jesus or of any other master is understood when the Life Jesus called the Father is realised. This could not be the product of the mind---a mere idea---but a living Consciousness in Life itself.

"When Jesus saw the imperfection in man he knew that man himself was the cause. Therefore without an understanding of what our background is, what we think and feel is merely a projection of that background. Without this self-knowledge, enlightenment is impossible.

"Unless the mind is freed from the ideas of what God is, there can be no realisation of the Real, there will merely be an idea of what Reality is and this is not the Truth, for when one idea is worn out a new one is created. The Real is beyond ideas, beyond the mind, and comes into being from within, not from without. It is only realised all the illusions of the mind are dissolved through understanding how they come about."

"I see," I said, "that the Yoga of the Christ is freedom from the self. When the self dies then God performs His own deeds and being the Creator of all things, having Intelligence beyond the mind of man, this Intelligence comes into operation when the mind ceases to formulate its own conclusions."

He replied: "Yes, my son, but this is merely an idea still. What you have said may be a truth but it is not the Truth. Truth can be experienced only when the mind is still, and I want you to experience that, for it is of great importance. An intellectual knowing is still mental, not spiritual. The Spiritual can come only through true meditation."

For some time we sat meditating, not on an idea or an image but seeing all that was not the Truth, seeing all the false, seeing the mind at work, knowing its movements, its cherished hopes and ideals. All these things were now dissolving away as I saw that they were merely a projection of the self and "BEING" was being realised more and more.

All Power, all Intelligence, all Love was there waiting to operate as the self died, for only the self stood in the way.

* * * * * * *

Chapter IX

I don't know how long I was in this state of bliss; all I knew was in this state of bliss; all I knew was a stillness that I did not create, a silence that came into being, and in that silence was the Eternal Creativeness.

Words cannot explain this state. The "I" has dissolved away in the great "I AM". The Father was operating through the temple He created for that purpose. All Power, all Wisdom, all Love was Eternal, Ever-present.

I knew that the self was nothing and could do nothing by itself, that it had no power of its own.

I was content, for all struggle had ceased. The Uncreated alone was creative. My thoughts and images of the past were dissolved in the living Present that was always new, the living moment that was Real. I knew now what my friend meant by the self being freed from its own bondage. I could write millions of words about it but even that would not reveal this ecstasy of BEING that was beyond mental formulations.

CHAPTER X

I HAD a feeling of satisfaction as we came back down the valley towards the sanctuary. My friend must have sensed my thoughts for he said:

"I am much pleased with your progress, it has been smooth and harmonious, and I will be very sorry when the time comes for you to leave."

I replied: "I feel the same way and am grateful for your kindness and consideration and Love which I appreciate more than words can tell. But I still feel that I am not worthy"...I had hardly finished when he spoke again:

"Whether you are worthy or not does not matter. Those who give to the world great things never think whether they are worthy or not. They realise that they are channels through which the Intelligence manifests. It did not enter their minds whether they were worthy or not. Jesus said, 'Know ye not I am in the Father and the Father is in me.' But you have at the back of your mind an idea of your unworthiness. If you can see now that this idea is merely the result of your background, your conditioning, you will not think that way again."

I knew it was a rap over the knuckles but it was said with compassion and love, and I realised how stupid I was. I was still caught up in the conditioning of the words which were so often said to me when a boy: "You should be seen and not heard." I was no longer bound by that feeling; it disappeared there and then.

In fact it was not the first time I had been checked about this. The Hermit of Ling-Shi- La quietly and gently rebuked me when he said: "We are not concerned with your worthiness; we are concerned only with how the Truth can best be made known to the world. You are a good instrument and we know that you will be a better one after this."

When we reached the sanctuary Norbu was waiting on the doorstep to meet us. She was radiant. She wore a red woollen jacket with green and white checks which she had made herself, and in her hair she wore her favourite wild poppy.

Her face was radiant with happiness and she smiled with her eyes and beautifully formed mouth.

I said to her: "You are a real beauty today, Norbu. Is this for my benefit?" My friend chipped in: "I think this is getting rather serious."

At the back of his mind he knew that there was a latent deep affection that could be fanned into a living fire any moment and knowing that one day there must be a parting he was concerned lest that parting would be made difficult. I knew this too, for I have a great capacity to love and felt at that moment I could put my arms around Norbu.

I took her hand in mine in front of my friend and said: "I love you very much, Norbu, and I always will."

Tears came into her smiling eyes and she said: "I love you too very much and I will miss you terribly when you leave us. But I will not be sad for I know you have work to do and I will have the memory of your life with us."

I knew then that everything was well and I took her in my arms and asked my friend to bless us.

The he said: "This is my command, you are to love one another as I love you." We knew what that meant, it meant a true spiritual Love beyond the physical.

We sat down to lunch and the talk was animated with Life and laughter. There was that happy carefree feeling accomplished by a bond of Love that united the three of us, that seemed ageless.

In the afternoon Norbu came in and sat down with us, for she was an adept in her own way, and I knew that she benefited much from our discussions as he called them.

My friend never implied that he was my teacher, or my master; this was his way of revealing the false, so that we could realise the truth ourselves.

My friend started again with the words: "This is my command, you are to love one another as I have loved you," looking at us both. "These are the words of the Master Jesus and they are also my words for both of you."

"The Yoga of the Christ is freedom," he said, "freedom comes when all the false, all the me---the I---the self---is understood, for they are the same. When the me---the I---the self is not understood, when it does not know and is caught up in its hopes and its desires, there is always the reaching out in trying to overcome again and again, and this makes freedom impossible, but, through understanding, overcoming becomes unnecessary, You understand that now, don't you."

"Yes," we replied, like one person.

Then he continued: "When you conquer one desire, you have to conquer it again and again. It is the same with your enemy, you have to conquer him again and again, that is why we always have wars. The moment you overcome one desire there is another desire to be over- come, so that which is overcome is never understood.

"In fact you will see now all that overcoming is merely a form of suppression and you can never understand that which you suppress. Therefore you can never be free from that which you repress. You have just recently experienced that, have you not? There is no longer the repression of your affections, but there is now freedom with your affection which makes it more alive with Love. For when there is true Love there is no desire, there is but the expression of that Love in freedom."

Norbu replied: "I know that now, Master, I know I can love now with all my heart and because I love with all my heart and not with my mind, I am free from desire. Master, you have shown me the way to love."

"No, my dear," he replied, "you found that out for yourself. I could not have shown it to you because you can experience that only by yourself. It must be your own experience, not mine."

I knew that freedom too, and have, ever since then, known that love of the heart frees you, while love of the mind binds you. Love of the heart is giving, while Love of the mind is desiring. There is a great difference between the two, one is of God, the other is of the self. The Love of God lives for ever, It is Eternal, while the love of the self dies with the self; it is but a shadow of love, as the self is but a shadow of the real.

But you can never know true love unless you love someone with all your heart and soul, then you know what love means. The overcoming of fear is merely the postponement of fear, is it not? What is it that most people fear?"

I replied: "I should say that most people fear death. Jesus said that was the last fear that man must free himself from. In other words he meant that when one was freed from the fear of death he was really free."

"Yes, that is true. The greatest fear is the fear of death and *the problem now before us is not how to overcome the fear of death but to understand the whole meaning of death.* This does not only apply to the old but to everyone, young and old.

"It is not merely adhering to a belief whether one continues to love or does not continue to love that solves the problem.

"There are some who say they are spiritual beings, and some say they are not spiritual beings and there is nothing afterwards. They say they are merely the product of environment. But both are thinking-believing and that does not solve the problem either.

"Now, what is it that makes people crave to continue and what is it that continues? What they want to continue is a name, form, experience-knowledge-memories. That is what the self is, what the me is, what the I is, for they are virtually the same, and that is what they want to continue. If you will look carefully you will see how true it is.

"You realise now that you are your memories, your experiences, your thoughts, and at whatever level you place your thought process you are still that, and you are afraid that when death comes that process which is you will come to an end, or you may believe that you will continue in some form after death and come back again in the next life. This you will see is but an expression of your belief, it is part of your mental process. I am not saying that there is not an after-Life but the mere idea of It does not solve the problem.

"Life-Spirit obviously cannot continue because it is beyond mind, beyond time. Continuity implies time---yesterday, today, tomorrow. Therefore that which is timeless can have no continuity; only that which is of time has continuity. That which is eternal and ever- present has no beginning and no ending, therefore has no continuity.

"You can only express what you know, your thoughts, your

memories, your knowledge, your experience. You cannot express what you do not know, you can only express what is in your mind. You cannot express what is beyond your mind, you cannot express Reality, for you do not know what it is. When the mind becomes quiet through this understanding, then that which is Real-Eternal is realised and Its operation is wide and unlimited.

"To say that I am a spiritual entity is a comforting thought, but, in the process of thinking about it, it is caught up in time, is it not? Therefore it cannot be Timeless! And therefore is not Spiritual. Time is relative, but the Timeless is beyond the relative and therefore is not subject to time, and being Unknown is not subject to the known; therefore it cannot be expressed as the known.

"What you want to continue is what you know. If you look carefully again you will see that it is not that which you don't know you want to continue. If you look clearly into this you will see the Truth of it. So what you have is merely your thinking-feeling and that is what you want to continue, because you know nothing else.

"As you do not know the Unknown, obviously it is the known you want to continue, so you are afraid it will come to an end. *But there is only Reality when that which continues comes to an end.* But you are afraid to end, so you are afraid of death, afraid to die. You want to carry on from yesterday to today-tomorrow, so you build up Utopias and sacrifice the living present to the future, liquidating people because of the desire to continue.

"Now that which continues obviously cannot renew itself. Only that which is ever- present, moment to moment, is reborn, renewed, moment to moment. In this there is no memory, no past, no future, no good, no evil.

"If we look into the problem closely we will see that what continues is memory in various forms and because you cling to memory you are afraid to die. Now you will see clearly that memory---the self being of time must die before there is *That* which is beyond Time.

"The mind cannot formulate or conceive That which is beyond time. It can know only that which is the result of time, of the past. What you read, what you think, what you believe, the mind formulates of yesterday, today and tomorrow but it cannot formulate moment to moment. To live in the ever-present there is no yesterday, today or tomorrow. There is only now. So the mind is afraid of coming to an end because it clings to yesterday, today and tomorrow, to its beliefs and its theories, and is not sure because it is liable to change from one idea to another.

"Your difficulty is to die to all you have accumulated, all your experiences of yesterday, to your beliefs, your ideas, your hopes. But that is death, is it not? That is what you die to.

"What you know can never reveal the Unknown which is beyond the known, beyond time. What you know is of time and time can never reveal the Timeless.

"Before I go farther I want to know if you understand this clearly."

I replied: "Yes, I do. When I die moment to moment to the things of the past, is there the Unknown, the Real. That which continues can never know the Truth---the Real---the Unknown---the New, it can only know its own projections. When you live in time, yesterday- tomorrow becomes more important than the Living Present which alone is creative. We must die to the moment that is past and live in the Living Present, then in death there is Life."

"Yes," said my friend, and he continued: "If you will look into you mind you will see that to live in the Living Present there cannot be a yesterday or a tomorrow. This is true activity-action, not reaction which is the result of memory, the result of yesterday. You will also note that there is no dead in the Living Present which is eternal. That is why Jesus said:

'Let the dead bury the dead.'

"CREATIVENESS IS LIFE IN ACTION. MAN DOES NOT CREATE LIFE, NO MORE THAN HE CAN CREATE GOD. *What he does do, is to create an idea of God, which he thinks is Truth, and not until he sees how stupid this is can he free himself from this illusion that blinds him to the Truth, Time cannot create Life, can it?"*

I replied: "I know of many who think that in time they can be creative. I realise that in time we can master a technique but that is not being creative."

"To master a technique," he said, "is merely habit, but habit is not creative, is it? There is always the conflict, the struggle in mastering a technique. Therefore a technique cannot be creative. As long as the self is in conflict with what it is doing, there cannot be a creative state. As long as the mind is caught up in opposites there will always be conflict and this denies creativeness."

"Then how is it possible to achieve creativeness?" I asked.

"It is not possible to achieve Creativeness," he replied, "what you must understand is that which denies Creativeness, and the understanding of this means the understanding of the self. When the mind is free from the demands of the self there is peace, and in that peace is Creativeness. It comes into being without effort or struggle because It is ever-present. Creativeness is from moment to moment. But you would like to hold Creativeness so that you would be able to express It. But this you cannot do, because Creativeness is beyond mind, beyond time. Therefore you have to cease functioning in time to become creative. When the self dies there is Life, so is there Creativeness. Jesus said, in other words, he who seeks to save *his* life (relative) will lose but he who gives up his life will retain It.

"Just as the lake is quiet when the wind ceases, so there is Creative Being when the problems of the mind come to an end.

"I of mine own self am nothing, it is the Spirit of the Father within me that doeth these things."

Then he closed his eyes as if in prayer and the words flowed from him without thought: "O Eternal Living Presence, I of myself am nothing, but with Thee I am all there is, for Thou art not divided.

"When I reasoned divinely and observed the false, I cleared the way for Thy Living Presence.

"In Thy Living Presence I was devoid of the sense of time because Thou art the Timeless One. Time, I saw, was of my own thought.

"I saw there could be no Reality in personality, because Thou alone are Real and indivisible.

"I saw there could be no Reality in sin, because Thou art all there is and there is no sin in Thee. Only in the mind of man does sin dwell and this is of his own making.

"Thou art the Truth and Truth is all there is, Thou art not divided because there is not anything that can divide Thee.

"Thou art unchangeable because there is not anything that can change Thee.

"When I saw that time blinded me to Thy Living Presence I died to yesterday. "Now , the Living Truth has set me free, knowing that the self is the error, believing the false to be the true. Now the self has died, Thy Life is mine for evermore, "O Blessed Eternal Living Presence."

* * * * * * *

As we looked upon his face we both saw the Master of Masters, his face enveloped in a light that was not of this world.

I took Norbu's hand in mine and we sat in that state of ecstasy, I don't know how long, for time had ceased to be. I knew then within me that there was no death, that death was swallowed up in Life Everlasting, and in that peace, in that silence, was the Real and the fear of death was no more.

CHAPTER XI

The days were creeping on and winter was beginning to show herself in real Tibetan style. Snow had fallen during the night and a blanket of snow covered Zamsar. From now onwards the blanket of snow would remain for at least six months, the sun was warm during the day but the night was below zero.

I was conscious of the fact that I must soon be on my way back to the world I came from, yet that world seemed to be so far away; I had entirely forgotten it during these last few months.

One thing I knew was that a great transformation had taken place. My changing ideas had disappeared, I was no longer changing from one idea to another about Truth. That stupid conflict was now dead, for I knew that even the most advanced idea was merely an idea and was not the Truth.

Immediately I saw this, all ideas about Truth disappeared. There was no longer a craving for the Spiritual or the material; I knew I could not possess either. In this pliability of mind there was freedom, and in freedom there was Truth, and in Truth there is Love.

Love is Truth, but we do not know what Truth is, so we do not know what Love is; we talk about Love, but that is not Love---it is merely our own mental creation, which is not Love. When we are thinking about Love it is not Love we are thinking about but a person we love. But do we love that person or do we merely possess that person?

When there is possessiveness there is jealousy and fear, and that is not love. When we find out what is not love, then we will experience Love. Surely Love does not mean possession, jealousy, fear. But, when you possess, there is fear, there is jealousy.

If you read aloud what I say you will experience transformation

121

that comes as a result of knowing yourself. You will see that which is not Love, and when that happens the false will fall away and Love will be immediate, because it is now and comes into operation when the way is made clear for It.

If you are married, have husbands, wives, children whom you possess, whom you use, of whom you are afraid or jealous, if you become aware of this you will see that that is not Love. Appeasement is not Love.

You give a coin to a beggar and walk on, is that Love? You may feel that you have done your good deed for the day, but is that Love? You may think you love mankind, but do you?

What we are doing is inquiring into the question of Love. When we inquire into the question of Love, we see what is not Love. Then we begin to understand ourselves in relation to Love. Then we begin to understand ourselves in relation to Love, and by doing so there is freedom from that which is not Love, and in this freedom there is Love, because you do not create Love.

You cannot possess Love. Love must possess you, and, when Love possesses you, you are no longer afraid or jealous or possessive.

When you are conscious of giving or receiving Love there is no Love. It is merely an expression of the mind and not of the heart.

Have you ever asked yourself what is the difference between yourself and the beggar? He may be in rags, you may have fine clothes. He may have nothing and you may have plenty, but that is merely a superficial difference. When you look more deeply, however, you will see that he is made the same way, is alive, the same Life is there, he is living as you are living. You are a beggar too, only on a higher level, nevertheless a beggar.

Strip yourself of your conditioning and the beggar of his condition and are you not the same? Is Life any different in you or in the beggar? It is; because of the society we create through our conditioning, this continues our conditioning.

You call it noble to give to charity, but you cannot call that love. Are you not still the central figure? You may sympathise with those who are conditioned, but is that Love? Who is the cause of this conditioning? You are, but we will not inquire into your motives and actions, you are afraid to do so, because it will upset you. You are afraid to look at yourselves. But unless you do, how can these conditions dissolve? Do you not perpetuate this condition through your own conditioning, when you do not know your conditioning?

You attack society for these conditions, but this is merely an escape, because you are afraid to inquire lest you find out what you really are like.

You do not care to be reminded of what you are like, so you sympathise with the victims of society, but are they not your victims? If you inquire you will see how you created this society.

Is forgiveness Love? You may think that you are a loving person because you forgive. But let us look at this problem of forgiveness. Why do you forgive? I insult you, you are hurt. You resent it, you remember it. Then you forgive. Why? Because you are still the central figure and this boosts your morale. But is that Love? You are still the important person, are you not? Love is not personal aggrandisement within or without. Love comes into being when the self has disappeared.

So you see that sympathy, forgiveness, possessiveness, jealousy, fear, is not love. One who loves is indifferent to all these things. As long as the mind is playing with Love, there is no Love; it only corrupts Love; it cannot give birth to Love, because it denies Love.

123

You write about Love but that is not Love; you talk about Love, but is that Love? You hear people talking about Love, but look and see if there is any Love in them.

When there *is* Love you never talk about it.

Love cannot be bought or sold. Love is beyond time. Only the things of time can be bought or sold. That is why our troubles, our miseries, multiply. The mind creates the problem and the mind tries to solve the problem, but you can see that this is impossible, because there is no Love. Only when the mind no longer has to solve the problem is there Love, and Love alone can solve the problem. When the mind is active you will see that the hearts is empty of Love. Yes, when the mind is active it fills the heart with things of the mind, the things of time. But Love is not of time; it comes into being when the things of time are silent. Therefore the solution of the problem is still the mind, to understand its ways, to see what we are, what we are doing; to see that we ourselves are the problem. But we are afraid to face the fact, and so the problem is never solved.

What do we do? We build churches, invent new organisations, we write, we preach, we adopt new slogans, we organise new political parties, we have conferences. We call ourselves this society and that society for world peace, world this and world that. But do we solve the problem? No! We only further complicate the problem.

When we see that the problem is the product of the mind, then to solve the problem the mind must cease to formulate new methods with the same old background. *Then* there is Love, and not before, and with Love all our problems are solved.

We talk about the practice of Brotherhood and Brotherly Love. We inaugurate societies. But this is still within the realm of the mind, is it not? When you understand all this, when all this racket has ceased, Love comes into being because It IS now, and we don't create it.

Then we will know what Love is. To say that you love the world has no meaning if you do not know how to Love "One". It is only when you truly love one, and in that Love you will know how to love the whole. It is because we do not know how to love one that our love for others is false. For when you truly love one, you love all. Then the heart is full and the mind ceases to formulate. In this is the solving of all our problems. Then we shall know why Jesus said: "Love your neighbour as yourself", for here lies our true happiness.

The lesson of Love was the greatest lesson I learned from my friend and from Geshi Rimpoche. These words of mine, I hope will open the way for you as their words opened the way for me.

* * * * * * * *

I said to my friend: "You have not mentioned that the day is drawing near when I shall leave you; I know you do not wish for me to go, but I must go; and I feel, that day is not far off."

"Yes," he said, "I was waiting for you to speak about it. In fact I put it into your mind so that it would come first from you and not from me. You know well that I shall miss you. In fact all of us will miss your presence in the flesh very much indeed, but, as you know, I shall be following you in your work in the world, for that is my work too. I will be by your side with your other helpers, some of whom have already left the physical.

"You are aware by now that most people live mostly in a superficial conscious state, merely a consciousness of their daily activities with the din of social problems and personal anxieties. Very few are aware of the deeper layer of consciousness that is influencing them according to their conditioning, because they are too busily occupied with their daily activities, their vanities, their cravings, hates, jealousies, and fear. They are unaware of their conditioning which is affecting their actions in their everyday living.

"Most people struggle for position, power, wealth and all that the physical can give, thereby creating further conditioning, and it is this deeper layer of conditioned consciousness that is projecting itself to the surface, causing all kinds of upheavals in mind and body.

"There are also those who divide the consciousness into the inferior and superior, and who say that the higher is the Spiritual entity. But is this not still a projection of their desire to become? It is merely a belief, you see; it is still of the mind, a mental formulation, is it not? This belief in a spiritual entity is an escape from their conditioning and can never relieve them of their conditioning, for their conditioning will remain till they see how they have conditioned themselves.

What I want you to see is the action of the mind and to understand it thoroughly. Without understanding the deeper phases of your own mental activity you will be caught up in your own ideas, and the ideas of others, which is the very thing I want you to avoid. So you see, no matter what you think or how you think about being a spiritual entity, it is still a product of your own thought-process, and therefore a product of time, and being a product of time it cannot be Timeless, and only in the Timeless is there Spiritual Being, which is *now!* and which you do not create or formulate, for it is beyond mind."

I was eager to grasp the great truth he was revealing to me, and ventured to say: "To de- condition myself, the whole hidden recesses of the subconscious, or whatever name you give it, must be understood and brought to the surface in some way or another and that must take a long time."

"Yes," he replied, "all this involved, obscure, perplexing confusion which is hidden memory must be understood. But time cannot be the means used in this revealing, because if this revealing will be of time it can never be the Timeless; therefore there must be another way which is not of time but immediate, and only when there is an immediate release is there the *Real*. So you see that analysis which is a method of time can never reveal the Timeless but merely creates further conditioning, as you will see as we progress.

"You see now, don't you, that it is memory that is the cause of your action. You want to become something; then this becoming strengthens memory, which is hiding the Real.

"Let us look at this mental process thoroughly. Firstly, you have this superficial layer in which most people live and react and know very little more. In the next layer you have memory. When you want to know anything, when you react to people and things, memory comes into operation, so you act, because without memory there would be no reaction, no action, would there? Your action is the result of memory, which is merely your guide at the moment, because you know little else. You are caught up in your memories and this is your conditioning, and so you act and react because of your conditioning. You see that, don't you?"

"Yes, I do. I see that plainly."

"Now suppose we get beyond memory to a deeper layer, we will arrive at a state of quiet, a sort of void, as it were. Now the whole, the totality, is consciousness, therefore the Consciousness permeates all these layers.

"When you want to become there must be action, and this action must be the result of your memory, because you know nothing else yet. You can only know when all this hidden conditioning is understood, and when it is all understood there is a silence that you do not create. There is no longer a stream of thought rising from memory into the superficial consciousness. As long as there is a stream of memories which is your conditioning rising to the superficial consciousness, there cannot be silence. You may force the superficial to be silent through suggestion or repetition, and the mind obeys for the moment, but still you have that conditioned memory which is confusion, fighting for acceptance and eventually you succumb to its influence. Do you follow me?"

"Yes, I am following," I said, "constant transformation is taking place."

I was seeing in the depths of my mind, but not yet completely. But I knew then that the whole process would be revealed and I was content to wait.

He continued, for he could read my mind like a book: "Now, as long as there is the desire to become, you see that you must, under such circumstances, strengthen the idea of the self---the me---the mine, therefore strengthen your conditioning, your memory---the self.

But the emptying of all these layers can come about only when there is no longer a desire to become. So what you must understand is the process of becoming, and becoming, as we already know, is going away from Reality. It is really strengthening that which is hiding the Real. When you become, you are on your own with your memory, and what you get is but ashes but not the Real. You may say God is your guide; this again is but a thought, as you will see if you look deep enough; it is merely your memory. Do you understand that?"

I did understand, the light was dawning very clearly now and I could understand the whole meaning of what he was showing me. My own mind was in a state of transformation.

"Life,' he said, "is not merely one branch of the tree; Life is all the branches of the tree and also that which gives life to the tree. Therefore you must understand the whole process of Life to understand the beauty and the greatness of Life.

"Now, you see, to know the whole state of your being you must know what it is made up of; you must become aware of all the forms of conditioning, not only the superficial, but the mental and so-called spiritual as well. And when the whole content of the subconscious is understood you will understand what memories are, what your thoughts are, your thoughts in regard to your family life, your racial ideals, your religious beliefs, all your various experiences---the whole lot! Then you will see that they are not Reality because you can look at them and know them. But you cannot know the Real, you can experience the operation of the Real only when all else is understood and dissolved.

"Let us look at the process of analysis. In analysis you try to unravel every memory, every response and the cause of that response and go into it fully to dissolve them, which would need infinite time, patience and care. This long fruitless process of analysis is a never- ending process of time and surely a process of time can never reveal the Timeless. So instead of deconditioning yourself you are further strengthening your conditioning. You see that, don't you?

"Now what do you do? You meet the present, the new with the memories, of the past, old memories, old traditions, old ideas, beliefs, and so forth, which is your conditioning, so you meet the present, the new with your conditioning."

"Yes, I said, "I can see that. I meet today with the response of yesterday."

"All right," he said, "you already know the old wornout method of analysis step by step, analysing each response, trying to dissolve one, then another, and so on. Don't you see, by using this method, that the very process of freeing yourself causes further conditioning, because you are still caught up in yesterday and will still meet tomorrow in the same way.

"Now, to be free there must be instant freedom, not freedom in time for that is binding; therefore you must approach the whole problem *without the element of time, without memory.* For regeneration, transformation is not a matter of time. It is now, at this very moment, But how is this to be? That is the question.

"If you follow me carefully you will yourself experience the complete cleansing of the mind.

"What happens now to your mind, when you see that your memories are of yesterday, and to meet the NEW you must meet it free from yesterday. Then the new---the Real--- is freed from yesterday. The Real is now. You do not create Reality; only memories are created and are a hindrance to the operation of Reality which is unlimited.

"Now, you see the state of your mind, there is no longer a clinging to yesterday, when you meet today. When you see the Truth of this, when you see what is false, it falls away. *It is only the Truth that de-conditions you completely. So when you see the Truth about the false you are de-conditioned immediately, is that not so?"*

"Yes," I said, "I experience that freedom now. There is no longer a desire for choice, there is no central image that I want to cling to, no desire to become. And as I see the Truth of this I am liberated from yesterday. The Ever-Present is Real to me now."

"Yes," he assented, "when you see the Truth about anything you no longer argue about that thing. When you see the truth about memory, about beliefs, about nationalities, without condemning, without criticising, and see the Truth that it is false---you are free from the whole issue.

"My son, it is the Truth that sets you free. To see the Truth about the false gives you immediate freedom, and in this freedom Reality comes into operation, unlimited and mighty is that operation. We the heart and mind are free through the Truth, the Truth about that which is false, then the Truth is! Because the Truth is, you do not create It."

At this moment I felt that freedom; the present was the Living Present freed from the past, always new.

To meet the new with yesterday, it would be the old; but when I saw this was my self and saw the falseness of it, my conditioning, which was my self, dissolved there and then. The nothingness of the self was realised and the Real came into Being *immediately.*

I knew what my friend meant, for I experienced that freedom from time, from the past. As I write these words I feel that you will also experience that freedom from the past, so that you will meet the new, moment to moment, and, in this, all is possible because you are not hindered by the past. It is the past, is it not, that troubles you? Because the past influences the present and is projected into the future. But the Real is greater than the past or the future. It is a Livingness that is ever-present.

The past influences the present when you do not know. You fear because of the past, you hate because of the past, because you do not know the falseness of it. When you see your conditioning and understand it, there is an immediate release from the past and the whole content of the mind into the deepest layer is laid bare. I knew now what the Hermit of Ling- Shi-La meant when he said that my friend would explain in detail what he had told me of the Whole.

Yes, this is truly the Yoga of the Christ--- *complete freedom.*

The son of man becomes the SON OF GOD!

CHAPTER XII

ALTHOUGH the valley was covered with snow we went up to our favourite spot beside the glacier. A cold wind was coming from Nyiblung Richung, yet we were impervious to the elements. At the same time I knew that the journey I would soon take back over the Himalayas in the middle of winter would be no picnic, for many persons had perished on the passes during snowstorms. But I knew that all would be well. I had that feeling of confidence which I gained on the way to the Hermit of Ling-Shi-La and that confidence had never left me. (See *Beyond the Himalayas,* Chapter X). Besides, I would be accompanied by my friend back to Tragtse Gompa, the Monastery high up on the mountainside where Geshi Rimpoche was waiting, and I was looking forward to seeing this great sage again.

When we came near the house I could hear Norbu playing her favourite guitar in her own mystic way. There was something alive about her playing that went straight to the heart. You could not tell what it was, but it left you with a deep feeling of wonderment; she was giving forth what her soul felt.

My friend said: "Listen to that! I have never heard Norbu playing with such depth of feeling; he soul is pouring forth her feelings tonight. No one would believe that she is self- taught. She is the musician and the music all in one. If she were in the West, thousands would flock to hear her sing and play, for she is a true creative artist."

I said: "She has to thank you for that."

"Not quite," he replied. "It is only since you came that she has blossomed out. You have aroused in her that tremendous force of Love, of mother, sweetheart and child, all rolled into one. And I have never seen such a complete change; she could almost be the Madonna." "Yes," I said, "she could. She is the most beautiful character I have ever met. I would love to take her to the world I know."

"And she would love to go with you, but that cannot be. You are undoubtedly twin souls and the time will come, perhaps not in this life but it will, when the twain shall meet again in more conterminous circumstances. And I want you to tell her that, it will lighten the pain she will have when you leave. It will sustain that beauty of Love which is seldom seen in any human being."

When we reached the porch Norbu came to meet us; she was more radiant than ever. I said: "Norbu, I just love your laying; you are a great artist, and I wish I could take you with me, but that, the Master says, is impossible at present. You know, Norbu, I love you very much and I want you to remember that. It is not a possessive love but a love that lights up the soul with that light which never dims. I want you to keep that flame always lit, for it is the Christ Spirit which dwells in all of us and binds us together.

"The Master will talk to you when I am not here, and remember there is no separation in Spirit."

"I have already found that out," she said. Then I told her what my friend said.

Her face was radiant, and as she smiled through her tears she said: "I know! I am content now; in spirit there is no separation."

The three of us sat around the log fire and my friend gave one of his most enlightening talks. It was meant not only for me but also for Norbu.

He began like Geshi Rimpoche did, telling me of my journey to come. In fact I felt as if it were Geshi Rimpoche himself who was speaking.

He commenced by saying: "It is now twenty-one weeks since I

met you at Kalimpong and exactly eight weeks today since you arrived at Zamsar. Yet it seems like a few days. A lot of work has been done in those weeks, for which I am very glad. By the time you reach Kalimpong again it will be exactly thirty weeks; that is how we have planned it.

"Norbu and I will accompany you as far as Tragtse Gompa, and there you will stay with Geshi Rimpoche for two weeks; then Geshi will accompany you to Ok Valley, where you will remain for another three weeks with Geshi Rimpoche and the Abbot. Geshi Rimpoche feels that he wants a little more time with you for further preparations, and then a special meeting will be arranged before you depart, when you will meet all your friends again: Tung La, Tsang Tapa, Malapa and Dar Tsang, and I will be there too. Geshi Rimpoche is desirous of having another meeting when the Hermit of Ling-Shi-La can come and speak to you as he did before. After this I will accompany you back to Kalimpong where I met you. Then you will be your own self physically, but not spiritually."

"Our love will go with you," he said looking at Norbu.

"Yes, indeed," she replied, "our loving thoughts will be with you always."

"And I will be sending my loving thoughts to you," I said, "and now that I can travel in the astral I will also visit you. This place holds living loving memories of our companionship, for it is here that I have learned to know what true Love means."

"Yes," said my friend, "the greatest thing in the world is Love; it is above all else. It is the key that opens all doors and solves all problems as well as giving you perfect freedom. Without Love your heart and mind become dull. You may be very active socially, you may give all your time to religious rites and so on, but if you have no love your virtue is still merely an idea, and all your activities without

Love can never enrich your life.

"Merely to say that you believe in God does not mean that you Love one another. Is it not so that those who say they believe in God have destroyed half the world and maimed millions of humans who are still suffering? Is there any love for those who are still the victims of these believers? I think not!"

He went on: "Religious intolerance is caused by believers, leading to religious wars. They talk of God but their hearts are empty of Love. It it not so that half the world does no live happily with the other half because they are believers?

"We can only live happily together when we are human beings; then we shall share the means of production in order to supply food, clothing and other necessities for all, without stint or selfishness.

"But what do we see? Millions of people having an idea of a super-intelligence which they call God. So they identify themselves with this idea. But this is merely a projection of their own thought-process, which can never know Love.

"When you really love one person you can love others. Then your heart is full of Love and is warm with affection towards everyone. When you have no affection you live on words, you are sustained by words, you worship

God the Father of All. Yet you retain your religious prejudices and class distinctions because the heart is empty and the mind full of ideas and beliefs.

"To understand, you must have Love in your heart, and this is not a mere statement but an everlasting truth. You cannot cultivate Love. It comes swiftly and directly when it is not hindered by the mind. When your heart is empty there is no communion between yourself and others.

"When there is no communion there is no love. When there is Love there is that warmth which kindles the heart and there is no need for psychology or philosophy, for Love is its own eternity.

"Love is the missing factor in most people's lives; they lack that tenderness, that kindliness, that mercy in relationship, and so they join a society for culture and world reconstruction which produces nothing---because they have nothing to give but words. The mind and heart are filled with plans for world reconstruction but empty of that one ingredient without which there is no solving of any problems. The problem is with relationship, not with systems, blue prints and so-called reforms. You have one reform after another. You form one organisation after another on the same lines of your previous failures, and this goes on incessantly because there is not that ingredient of goodwill and Love which alone can solve problems.

"Relationship is the key to the problem and there is no relationship without Love and goodwill. So relationship is the problem, not systems and reforms which end in further confusion. As long as relationship is not understood there can be no right action; there can be no solving of the problems which is of the self. There can be no relationship without self- knowledge. Only with knowledge of the self is there wisdom, and with wisdom there is Love.

"Without Love no problem can ever be solved, no matter how brilliant the mind may be. If there is no relationship with one another, we continue to create further confusion.

"You read books on Love and goodwill, and most of it is mere chatter and nonsense. You have to rediscover the real within yourself through acknowledging your empty mind and heart not merely hide behind a belief in God. It is only Creative Intelligence, Creative understanding, which will bring happiness and peace to the world, and who is the world? You and I and everyone like us, we are the world."

Then he said: "I have spoken to you both as if I were directly speaking to you so as to make you think for yourselves. Merely to speak about a third person takes away the effectiveness of your own transformation."

"Yes," I commented, "as you spoke, I had that deep discernment of my own conditioning."

"Yes," he said, "it is only-self knowledge that brings wisdom, and with wisdom you have Love, the key to all problems."

These talks together in the evening were the job of my life. They had the effect of making one see one's self without criticism, without condemnation or fear.

I looked at Norbu and said: "I shall envy you when I am not with you here to enjoy these nights of perfect companionship which have a most wonderful transforming effect on me."

"And on me," she replied. "I have never known what Love was till you came; it was like a flower coming into full bloom. We have sat here together listening and absorbing the great truth about Love, and now my heart is full of Love, for I know what it is to really love 'one'. Knowing that, I can now love and help others to understand as I understand."

Then she got up and busied herself with getting the supper ready.

It was a wonderful thing that we could all experience Love in perfect freedom without possessiveness, that we could bare our hearts without evasion or being self-conscious about it in any way, and I said so to my friend.

"Yes," he said, "we sustain the false by a belief in it, and thus we fail to understand ourselves. The cause of our unhappiness is the ignorant direction given to the mind which we embrace thereby failing to understand the cause of our misery. When this is understood there is immediate freedom.

"We formulate opinions, beliefs which can be changed and are changed as new knowledge is revealed. But that which is changeable is not Reality, for Reality is unchangeable. Reality-God-Love cannot be changed and is ever present within us. Yet we cannot realise this until we have discerned that the changeable is not Real.

"Although we improve by changing from our fixed ideas of sickness and death to those of health and Life, yet even this is of the mind. When you realise this, even these ideas and their opposites fall away and Reality comes into being without effort.

"Reality does not know good or evil, sickness or death; man alone creates these beliefs which bind him in sorrow and conflict.

"When you experience Truth-Reality through understanding yourself, you have no longer opinions about It. You know. But if you do not understand yourselves, how can you understand anything else? For the root of understanding is within you.

"To understand yourself you must understand your relationship with others, your reactions, your fears, your antagonisms, your beliefs and so on, and see how these come about. Through your reactions to another you can understand yourself through discerning your thought-feeling-reaction. When you understand yourself, you will see how you have been conditioned. You will see how you are reacting to protect your conditioning; you will know what your conditioning, your beliefs, your opinions, your fears, are; all of these have their roots in your mind only, and have no power except the power you yourself give them.

"If your mind is controlled by fixed ideas and beliefs, you will never know the Truth about anything, because you do not know what is false. But if your mind is flexible and free through understanding you will experience the True meaning because you will know the false. The false you create, the True you do not create, for It is Ever-Present. Then you will know your relationship with others, and with the world, for in you as in everyone else is the same Whole; you are the result of the Whole, not the result of a part of the Whole, because there is no division in Wholeness. This is the Reality about which you can have no opinion and no doubt; this understanding alone will bring the necessary and vital change in the individual first and then in the world, for the world is what individuals are. If you look deeply into this you will see that we make the world what it is. "As we sow, so do we reap". What the inner is, so will the outer be.

"Look into your mind and you will see it is your thought-feeling-reactions that make society what it is. Society is the projection of ourselves and so is the world.

"When you are brutal, antagonistic, perverse, greedy, envious, jealous, hateful, you create in body and in circumstances just what you are mentally.

"To study oneself requires complete honesty. You have to be aware of your thought- feeling-reaction, especially towards others, and then you will see what you are. You will see what is hiding Reality. You will see how much self is in front. Jesus said: 'Get ye behind me, Satan.' Satan represented the self, the liar, the cheat, that was hiding the Real.

"There is nothing to compare with the operation of the Real. It is Creative Wisdom, Love and Power, beyond the mind of man. When the false dies, the Real manifests, and then there is true relationship which means freedom and happiness, prosperity, love, affection.

"There is the hidden self that lurks in the deeper layers of the mind. It has been building up from infancy and most of our motives are hidden behind a series of misconceptions. This is the cause of inward confusion, resentment and prejudice. There is a fierce struggle between conflicting desires. We praise, we accept, we deny, we condemn, we criticise, all because of this conditioning which we believe to be real. Not until we have seen how false it is, and how it has come about, is there release from it. When the self sees the falseness of all this, which is merely the self, then it ceases to project itself because the self sees that the self is the cause. The self is the devil, but the self has to know this; then it no longer wants to project itself and therefore ceases to operate; then there is a silence that is not created. When the self ceases to operate, Reality---which is Love, Wisdom and Creativeness---comes into being without effort. Reality operates when the self gets out of the way. It is 'clear the way for the Lord.'

"Do you understand what I say?"

"Yes," I said, "I do understand very clearly now, much better than ever before. I can see that when I am aware of what is happening on the surface I can see what my mind is made up of; then the deeper layers give up their hidden conflicts and complex thought-feeling- reactions; and when this is understood the mind becomes silent without compulsion, and in this silence there is freedom. That which was hiding Reality now dissolves away and Reality *is.*"

"Yes, that is true, my son, but it must not be merely an intellectual knowing, it must be an active transformation. As the mind gives up its dead wood, Real Life will take its place. But if you merely spin words, then your mind will be full of ideas and your heart empty of Love."

"Yes," I said, "I can see that when you believe a certain way you

141

must discern why you believe in that way. If you are antagonistic to another belief you must also discern why. You will see that it is merely a matter of belief and is not Real. If you disbelieve you must deal with your disbelief in the same way. If you are prejudiced you must also understand why."

"Yes," he said, "there is no escape; you have to face the problem to understand it, even your most cherished ideals must be understood. Then you will see how you are conditioned, otherwise there can be no freedom. It is a thorough cleansing process that must be done and is sometimes difficult for the believer."

"I can see," I said, "that merely to control my thought-feeling, to apply a brake to it, merely to say that this is wrong and that that is right, is a waste of precious time; I must see how and why I am conditioned. If I am merely controlling my thought-feeling there can be no understanding. It is understanding of my conditioning that frees me."

"Yes, my son, that is true. Resisting, denying or accepting, only makes you more thoughtless, narrow and petty in an effort to protect your own conditioning; you struggle to protect your ignorance. But when you know the Truth about yourself the struggle ceases; then the mind becomes quiet, and in that quiet Reality is."

"I have experienced that now, and I understand it," I said.

"Yes, my son, you must look into your mind to see what is there; then it slows down itself. But if you use force or begin to analyse, you create opposites---and this only adds to the confusion. But if you discern any thought-feeling without restraint, without comparison, without judgment of right and wrong, seeing completely and impersonally what the mind is made up of, even your so-called higher thought (which is merely part of your thought-process), you will become aware of that which is without restraint, without judgment of right and wrong, without comparison, that which is unchanging. You will become aware of that which is significant, that which is Real, Eternal, Ever-Present, beyond all thought-processes.

"You must follow this up with awareness of the Real, not as a separate entity but as the whole. This will give perfect freedom, free from mental confusion, beliefs, opinions and separation. You will know the Yoga of the Christ just as the Master himself did. The Father who ever remains within will operate, performing His own deeds and not your conditioning which is stupid, petty and narrow.

"Being religious in the fundamental sense of the word is the Yoga of the Christ, no dependent on a particular organised religion, for this will make you irreligious---which leads to separation and strife through your beliefs.

"Separation has been responsible for dissension, economic disasters, wars, starvation, oppression; and man himself is the cause. He has only to look into his own mind and see the cause, 'separation', staring him straight in the face.

"Man labels himself with names, yet there is only one Life that supports all. When you understand this you will understand the Man who showed mercy, compassion to all, and refused to be limited by any nation, dogma or society.

"True religion, my son, is above all creeds, nationalities and ideals. To know this is the beginning of the realisation of the One-in-All and the All-in-One. It is the way to world peace and prosperity, and happiness for the individual. For when we become truly religious in the true sense of the word, there will be peace in the soul and peace in the world as a result. There must be that inward peace in the world as the result. There must be that inward peace, that wisdom and Love of the Christ-Spirit that awakens in all souls that

143

are freed from separation."

"Yes," I said, "the words of the Master sum up the ways of those who merely preach separation and creed: "Yes, it was about you, you hypocrites indeed, of whom Isaiah prophesied as it is written, "This people honour me with their lips but their heart is far away from me. Vain is their worship of me, for the doctrines they teach are but human precepts"".

"Yes, my son," he replied, "Jesus was showing the unreality of tradition, creed and dogma which mean so much to most people and which are devastating them today. They are ignorant of it because they are caught up in it. People worship pomp, ceremony and tradition, but that which they worship destroys them. It is merely lip service where love and affection are sadly lacking, while separation, antagonism, strife, war and misery are in evidence.

"Right thinking can come only when you see the false, when the false is understood and truth about the false is known; and the truth about the false is that it is false. When this is known, right thinking is possible. Right thinking is freedom, conditioned thinking is oppression."

"Yes," I said, "I can see that only Love can solve our problems. These can never be solved by psychology or philosophy, systems or ideals, which we indulge in; these are the things of the mind. We are still caught up in separation and distrust of one another. We see this daily but few comprehend the danger in it. Most people are bound by nationalities, by religious beliefs, by political ideals, which men follow blindly, and so like sheep they are led to the slaughter."

"Yes, my son, but there is more to it than that. For only through being aware of the self and what it is, do you discover your conditioned thought. You must see that you are merely copying another, that you are not yet able to think for yourself but have acquired a habit of thinking with antagonism, which is disastrous to yourself and others.

"You must see things as they are, in their true perspective. Then there is no confusion in the mind that has truly discerned what the mind is made up of. When these things of the mind are laid aside, the Ever-Present Reality which is Wisdom and Love will come into being in the hearts of all mankind."

I felt I was in the presence of the Christ, as he closed his eyes and said these words in a deep subdued voice with great meaning:

"He who has sent me is at my side.

"He has not left me alone for I always do what pleases Him.

'I AM THAT I AM'

"On the many branches of my Tree of Life I have sung my song of Love.

"As my song was echoed in the green leaves, those who heard me realised their Oneness with me. Then my Life alone was food for them.

"All through the centuries of time my Timeless state remains. That is why sleeping souls in the world of time can still awaken unto me.

"The rhythm of my song stirs the hearts awaiting to hear my voice calling

'Come into my Cosmic Freedom'.

"So I arose and went. "I arose and went."

* * * * * * * *

As he spoke those last words Norbu was at my side, and as I took her had in mine we looked into his face and there we could see the face of the Master himself, shining like the sun. It was an experience I will never forget.

It was like the Last Supper, and it was for me, for we were to start the following morning on our long journey back across the Himalayas. It was the benediction to a wonderful stay at the Hermitage of Zamsar. How I wished I could stay there always, that was my thought. My friend had read it, for he said:

"There is nothing in the world we desire more than that you should stay here with us always, but as you know,there are higher beings than us, and in whom the same Life flows, who are guiding this work, and in the end a great blessing will come to us for putting the higher things before our own personal desires."

We sat down to the last supper we should have together. We all knew it, and yet we were very happy.

Norbu had prepared one of her special dishes of cold-jellied chicken and hard-boiled eggs, special bread that she had made herself, and fresh yak butter just out of the churn

After supper we sat up later than on other nights, even though we were to start early in the morning. I felt I could sit up all night--- and I think my friend and Norbu felt the same. Norbu played her favourite tunes on her guitar and sang her own love song that she had composed herself. I can hear it even now (and it is many years ago) so beautifully did she play and sing. She was a born creative artist; she played and sang by ear, and her music was creative and original, with great depth of meaning. It had all the colour of the spheres in it.

The fire was burning down, sending a red glow all over the

room, and a peace came over the whole scene, as we three sat close together, thinking of tomorrow, thinking of the vacant place that could never be filled, as

Norbu put it.

There was a silence as all our thoughts were in the one direction, a realising of the parting that was so near, yet a knowing that there was no parting in the Christ Spirit which is One in every living soul. This linked us together, and our memories would be as fresh as the morning dew.

My friend got up and said he was going to prepare for the morrow. Norbu then came close beside me and placed her head on my shoulder. It was the first time she had done this and there was a feeling of contentment, the fulfilment of a longing, and I felt it. She fell asleep and in a few moments I had fallen asleep too. I don't know how long it was, a moment, or an hour or a century, and when I awakened I thought I had slept through the ages. It was a most wonderful experience. We seemed to awaken together.

My friend was standing there, smiling upon us, and said: "My children, you have experienced an out-of-the-body state together which is perfect bliss; that is the state you are in when you leave the body; you embraced a soul-experience in a higher state. The expression of your desire has been consummated spiritually but you can bring back with you only a fragment of what it is really like.

"I watched you both leave the body at the same time, and come back at the same time, and you experienced identically the same thing, the consummation and culmination of your desire in the soul-state. That can be the ecstasy which all will experience when the Life Force in the body has risen to its Spiritual Source."

Norbu said that she had now a contented happiness that could not be defined; there was no more thinking of the parting---that had vanished. It was the result of the soul's embrace, and the desire to maintain the physical contact had disappeared.

That experience is possible to all when the heart is filled full with Love and the mind is emptied of possessiveness.

True Love is giving and receiving without being conscious of it. It can only be experienced to be realised. But all my words can never explain the unexplainable.

"It was truly a benediction of the Living Presence," said my friend, and the culmination of his efforts was crowned with exaltation. This is the highest attainment of the Yoga --- the Yoga of the Christ.

CHAPTER XIII

The clear, cloudless blue sky overhead was filled with millions of twinkling stars that lit up, in relief, the valley and the mountains, now covered with the winter snows. The sun had not yet risen, and, as I looked upon the enchanting and familiar scene, the white mountains stood out in relief against the dark blue morning sky like giant sentinels. So close did they seem, I felt that I could stretch out my hand and touch them, while the whole valley and the glacier covered in a snow blanket appeared as through a veil of subdued daylight.

I stood there watching the first rays of the sun strike the peak of Nyiblung Richung. The stars became fainter as the rays of the sun shone more and more on that never-to-be- forgotten peak upon which I had proudly stood a few weeks ago. The sun was gradually rising behind the mountains and soon the rays would strike the front portals of the Sanctuary. I was deep in thought, for my mind held lovely memories of all that had happened here.

As I stood gazing upon this wonderful scene of changing colours the deep red rays of the sun were turning to orange, and all the peaks began to reflect the colours as if they were on fire. As the first rays of the sun struck the Sanctuary I was conscious of someone beside me. My friend was standing there. He put his arm around my shoulder and said: "I hoped it would be like this, this morning."

I said: "I shall always remember it. I feel a tinge of sorrow that I must leave you and leave all that meant so much to me. The one consolation I have is that you will be still with me even after I go back over the Himalayas into that world that today seems so very far away."

Just then Norbu called us to breakfast by sounding the familiar gong that echoed up and down the valley as if the mountains were calling to me, the boom-boom of the echoing sound saying: "Don't go, don't go."

Then Norbu came out to where we were standing. She was radiant; her cheeks, rose- pink from the crisp air, matched her red jersey which suited her so perfectly and I told her so.

I said: "Did you see the sun rising this morning?"

"Yes," she said, "I was behind you, but I did not want to disturb you, because I saw you were in deep thought."

"Yes, Norbu, but you were part of the whole scene; you fitted into it so wonderfully. The mountains, the valleys, the silvery moon, the stars, the rising and the setting of the sun, yes, Norbu, I placed you there, and in my heart I shall remember you always."

Tears welled up in her lovely big blue eyes, and as she smiled through them her face lit up with the light of happiness, and I knew what her heart was saying, for it was filled full of Love.

After breakfast Das Tsering, the headman of the town, came up with the ponies and the little black stallion, which I had named Black Prince and which I would now be taking back to its real owner. Norbu's father had brought her beautiful chestnut mare on which I saw her on the way to Lhasa; it was full of spirit and tugged at the rein when it saw her. My friend took his familiar pony and led the one he picked up at Pede Dzong as a spare pack-pony. Das Tsering had a big brown pony and a pack-mule that came on behind.

He said: "I am coming with you to help in any way I can." I asked him in Tibetan: "How is the wife and baby?"

"Fine," he replied in the same language, looking at my friend in a grateful way, for it was he who delivered the baby boy.

So we started off on the journey, My friend went first, Norbu came next, I next, and Das Tsering took up the rear. It was cold when we started but as the sun rose it became quite hot. The rays of the sun reflecting on the snow make your eyes sore, so I wore the rayban glasses I had brought with me.

Norbu rode astride and a lovely rider she was. She seemed to be part of her pony as she rode up and down the steep inclines along the Kya Chu. This river in summer is fast flowing because of the melted snow and ice of the mountain swelling it, but in winter---what a contrast! It was frozen over in the calm and shallow parts.

We reached Dechen Dzong that afternoon about four o'clock. We had done considerably well, even though the track was covered with snow nearly all the way. Crossing the passes in snowstorms is dangerous in winter; and the danger in the spring and summer is swollen rivers from the melting snow and ice. Many Tibetans have lost their lives in this way, just as people in the West lose their lives through motor accidents. In Tibet people lose their lives in the rivers and on the passes, but no notice of fatalities seems to be taken by anybody except relatives.

We stayed the night at Dechen Dzong in the house of the headman whom my friend knew very well, and we were treated like lords.

Dechen Dzong is situated where the Dinga Lhe flows into the Kya Chu. There is a bamboo bridge over the Dinga Lhe but we did not use it, as the river here was shallow and frozen over and we crossed easily.

The following day we reached a place called Zenshi. In this part of the country there is a great valley very rich (as described in Chapter III). Here Norbu had an uncle and aunt who were the leading traders in the district. They owned several trains of yaks and donkeys, about

2,000 of these animals. Some of the Tibetan traders are quite wealthy. In transporting goods they take part of the goods as payment, so their stores cost them very little.

Tragtse Gompa, the Monastery where Geshi Rimpoche was waiting for us, was about three miles away. So my friend and I went on to the Monastery, and Norbu stayed with her relatives.

As we were nearing the Monastery I felt that delighted feeling of anticipation about meeting Geshi Rimpoche again. To be in his presence and to listen to his pearls of wisdom was real joy. When we reached the foot of the mountain on which the Monastery was built we were met by several Lamas, whom the Abbot had sent to help us up with our packs. We left our ponies in the stables below and then proceeded to climb the many steps hewn out of the rock- face.

When we reached about half-way up I could see Geshi Rimpoche and the Abbot coming down to meet us. The happy greeting I had from Geshi Rimpoche I will always remember. He told me that he had been impatiently waiting for me; I was his beloved son, and he had come all the way so that he would be with me on the way back to Ok valley.

I said: "I have been longing to see you too in the flesh and to hear you speak to me again. There is also a lovely girl who wants to meet you, for I have talked to her about you such a lot."

He replied: "Yes, I know, and her name is Norbu ('precious jewel')' You must bring her to me."

"So you know her?"

"Oh yes, my son, you know I am watching over you and know all about you." (I had forgotten for the moment that Geshi Rimpoche could travel in the astral.)

So one day we brought Norbu to see Geshi Rimpoche. When she saw him she took up the hem of his cloak and held it to her lips and he blessed her saying: "Arise my child; I am delighted with you; you have a wonderful future. It is not only men who are Yoga Masters, Norbu."

It was a real blessing for Norbu to know this. I was so glad for her sake and spontaneously kissed her in front of Geshi Rimpoche, my friend and the Abbot; it all happened so naturally. Geshi Rimpoche saw the spontaneous action and said: "God bless you, my children."

Then my friend spoke the same words that he said to me before: "It is the Love of God that unites us all together to do His Will."

Geshi Rimpoche then took all of us into his Sanctuary and gave us one of his wonderful instructive talks. I could listen to his voice for hours and was sorry when he finished.

He commenced with these words: "What I am going to say is applicable to all people irrespective of who they are or their station in life, whether rich or poor, whether titled or otherwise.

"There seems on the surface to be inequality between man and woman, man and man and woman and woman, but in Love, in Reality, there is none.

"We all have our suffering, our problems, we are burdened with worries, sorrow and joys, meeting and parting, sickness and health; these we all have with us. All people, no matter who and what they are, want to be free, and all are seeking a way out; we are all the same, there is no difference.

"Now, if we are in sorrow and suffering, to try to escape from it only increases the burden. Sorrow and suffering cannot be understood through an escape. It can be understood only through loving and understanding. You understand persons when you love them; you can understand anything when you love it. But we can be carried away by the word 'love' when the mind is chattering and the heart empty of Love.

"When you love someone is there any nationality? Is there any inequality? When the heart is empty, types become very important. We divide human beings into classes, nationalities, but when you love is there any difference? When the heart is generous there is no difference; you give of yourself. To one who is really seeking the truth, there is no difference, because Truth is to know Love. But if you continue to pursue a path there can be no Love, for the path means exclusion, and Truth is all-inclusive. To appeal to one section as against another is the cheap trick of a politician and the immature.

"We can understand a thing when we face it, when we do not want an escape. When we are free from escapes we understand. To be happy is to Love, to Love is to be happy. Then there is no division, no separation because Love bridges time and distance. When we love there is a sense of richness, and we are willing to share everything. When the heart is full, the things of the mind that divide us dissolve away.

"The mind is filled with blue prints for world reform, religious rites, chastity and virtue, but without the one resolving element of love there can be no true relationship. Do what you will, withdraw to the mountains, sit on a hill-top or live in isolation, as long as relationship is not understood there can be no right action. Therefore your problem is with relationship, and there is no relationship without self-knowledge. There is no escape from relationship---you may withdraw to the jungle or to the mountains---but you will still be related. In relationship you understand yourself; you can see how you think, feel and act. Thought must know its own activity, its own action.

"There is religion, there is chastity, only when there is Love. When there is true Love, chastity is not a problem. Without Love you pursue ideas of chastity. When there is Love and not the mere ideal of chastity, which is of the mind, the problem of chastity is solved.

"The nourishing of the heart is not a process of the mind, but when the operation of the mind is understood then Love comes into being. Love is not a word, the word 'Love' is not Love; when you speak of Love you will see that it is merely of the mind. When you realise that the word is not the thing itself then the mind, with all its rights and wrongs, its virtues and other qualities, ceases to interfere. Then there is Love that is not created in the mind but is *ever new, ever fresh*; in this alone there is virtue, chastity."

Then he opened his eyes and said: "You understand me now, don't you?"

I said: "Yes, perfectly, there is no problem when Love is ever fresh, ever new. It is when the mind tries to form ideas of what Love should be that Love loses its Reality."

"Yes, my son, that is the Truth that sets you free."

I could see the great wisdom of Geshi Rimpoche. He was showing us the Reality of Love, not the mere idea of Love with all its repressions, its suppressions and its so-called virtues, and that chastity of the mind was not Love---it was merely suppression of the sex urge without understanding. But when relationship was understood the mind saw its own formulations and ceased to interfere; then Love that is ever new, ever fresh and not of the mind but of the heart, came into being.

We do not create Love; Love is ever-present and comes into being when we understand that it is not made up in the mind. When the mind sees that it cannot create Love but only ideas about what

Love should be, then it becomes silent and *Love is.* Then there is no problem, for all problems are solved in Love. For Love is God and God is Love, and there is nothing else, all else is but an illusion of the mind, and when the mind is understood the illusion falls away; then Love worketh Its own perfection, for It is Its own Eternity.

There was always something rare about what Geshi Rimpoche said. He went straight to the heart of the problem, and we all knew it. It was the transforming action, the deeper meaning of the word, that was taking place; and, though I may have heard similar words before, they still had a transforming effect, even now. That is the beauty of Truth, it is always new.

Food was provided for us all in the Abbot's apartments and we sat down at the same table. The Abbot, the host, sat at the top; at his right sat Geshi Rimpoche and on his left my friend. Norbu and I sat at the other side opposite the Abbot.

"Would you like to remain a few days with us?" and he looked at the Abbot for his sanction. I could see that the Abbot was agreeable, though it was not customary to have a girl at the Monastery. Norbu jumped at the opportunity to be with Tibet's greatest sage; it was a great honour.

It happened that Norbu remained four days with us before she and my friend started their way back to Zamsar. During these days Geshi Rimpoche was at his best. I never saw him in such high spirits.

The day came for my friend and Norbu to leave. Geshi Rimpoche and I accompanied them on our ponies as far as Zenshi.

I can well remember the embrace Norbu gave me that morning. I saw the quiver of her lips as she smiled through her tear-filled eyes. Geshi Rimpoche then put his hand on my shoulder and said: "This is my beloved son and I will have to part with him too in the flesh, and you are my beloved daughter, Norbu."

Then he took her hand and put it into mine, saying: "God has bound us all together for His own purpose, and His Life unites us in one grand chain of everlasting Love in which there is no separation."

I knew that I would see my friend again at Ok Valley and that he would accompany me as far as Kalimpong on my way back, and as he put his arm around my shoulder in his usual loving way he said: "I will be with you again soon, my son," and then they departed on their way back to Zamsar. We stood and watched them. They looked back several times and waved till they were out of sight.

I felt I had taken with me something of that which I left behind, something which would always be fresh as the morning dew. Geshi Rimpoche could read my thoughts, for he said: "Love is God and God is Love, and God does not die or fade away. His Love is always fresh and new and is beyond time and space."

When we reached the Monastery late in the afternoon the Abbot was waiting for us. He also spoke of the beautiful soul of Norbu which shone out of her face.

Geshi Rimpoche said: "I doubt if greater beauty is to be found in all Asia."

The influence of Norbu was impressed on all who met her and left a memory that never faded as the years rolled by.

During the next week Geshi Rimpoche and I walked and talked every day about the work I had to do, and I listened to his advice. I loved every moment of his presence, a presence which was uplifting even when no words were spoken.

I asked him one day: "Why is it that I have to leave all those I love so dearly?"

Then he stood and looked at me and said: "God so loved the world that He sent His son into the world so that those who would listen would see the false and thereby know what is True. And the Truth would set them free. You must love the world, my son, just as the greatest of all Masters did. And those who hearkened unto Him became sons and daughters of God, not born of the flesh or the will of man but born of the Ever-Present Spirit of God which liveth now and forever in Love beyond time and space."

CHAPTER XIV

TRAGSTE GOMPA is one of the most beautiful Monasteries in Tibet. Perched high on the mountain, it faced down the valley of the Tobing Chu, which was now covered with snow. In the distance we could see the golden roof of the Potala at Lhasa, glittering in the sun.

At this time of the year the nights are cold and everything freezes after sunset.The blue sky is generally cloudless and lit up with millions of twinkling stars which reflect upon the crystal crisp snow, casting a veiled daylight appearance over the whole valley. There are also periods when the snow falls, with high winds creating blizzards, and the snow is piled up in parts more than ten feet deep. When these blizzards occur, you can hardly see even a few yards in front of you.

Every day we could see trains of yak and donkeys trudging up and down the valley, carrying the loads in and out of Tibet. Winter and summer this goes on as regular as clockwork, irrespective of whether there are blizzards, sunshine or rain.

I knew that one day I would also be making my journey back to Ok Valley, and then going on to Lingmatang and Kalimpong, a distance of about 2000 miles. The journey to Ok Valley would begin in about a fortnight's time, over rivers and passes covered with ice and snow.

When Geshi Rimpoche travelled in winter he had a number of others with him on yaks. the yaks go in front and make a track in the snow. The yak is the best snow plough on the Himalayan passes. A few yaks trudging through the snow soon make a path over the treacherous passes.

We had already agreed that we would by-pass Lhasa on our way back, as nothing could be gained by wasting time on a few officials who thought themselves Christmas!

So when the day came for us to start on our journey we were in high spirits. We made our way down the steep steps from the Monastery to where our animals were waiting for us.

The trade route ran along the Kya Chu at the point where it joins the Tobing Chu. We branched off to the right, cutting out the triangle between the Tobing Chu and the Kyi Chu, and we carried along the route (not the trade-route) to a place called Nampa. Although this route is not used very much it was quite good. It cuts off Lhasa, which is situated at the point of the triangle where the Tobing Chu and the Kyi Chu meet. We crossed the Lungsang Pass and reached the Kyi Chu about ten miles farther on than Lhasa, thus saving about twenty miles of difficult travelling, as the trade route in the winter is very slushy.

We reached the Jongto Gompa about four o'clock the second day, where we rested for the night. (Gompa means Monastery.) This route also saved us crossing the Kyi Chu, which is dangerous in winter, some parts being frozen over and other parts not. We had taken a completely unorthodox route by by-passing Lhasa, but time and energy were more important to us than officials who knew little or nothing of Truth. In fact they were devoid of Truth, being caught up in tradition and ritual.

The next day we reached a place called the Chu-Shur Valley. Here the Kyi Chu spreads itself out, creating many islands, at places it is more than two miles wide. In the village of the Chu-Shur there is a prayer wall about fifty yards long with many coloured deities carved on it. This valley is also very fertile, but it was now covered with a winter blanket of snow.

We crossed the Kamba La, a pass that leads up from the side of the river, zig-zagging up and down, and then we reached the Chaksam Ferry. Here we stayed at a beautiful Monastery, up on the right side, on the hill called Chokoryangtse Gompa.

Geshi Rimpoche was well known to the Abbot and we were given very comfortable quarters. I was glad of the complete rest overnight.

Next morning we crossed the ferry to the Ok side of the Tsang Po and began to climb the Nyapso La, a pass about 17,000 feet high. When we reached the top of the Nyapso La we could see way down the Tsang Po valley; the great Brahmaputra could be seen winding its way through the snow, the mountains on each side standing like silent sentinels looking down through the ages at this swift-flowing river, said to be the most holy in all the world.

Miles away I could see in the distance the turquoise lake called Yamdrok and the town of Pede Dzong. Geshi Rimpoche told me that we would stay there that night, for I had with me the headman's pony which I was returning. When we arrived, there was great jubilation. I thought the welcome given to my friend was wonderful but that given to Geshi Rimpoche was even more wonderful. A meal was prepared for us, and we accepted the kind offer of accommodation for the night.

When I told the headman that I had brought back the pony that he had so kindly lent to me he told me to keep it until I had finished my journey and it would be brought back to him later. I was delighted, to say the least, because Black Prince had become very dear to me; we knew each other so well now, and I would not have liked to change to another pony at this stage. Geshi Rimpoche thanked the headman and said: "I will see that your pony will be returned to you."

A sumptuous meal was prepared; I don't remember how many courses, but there were at least ten.

First we had minced meat in pastry, then slices of fish with pickled onions, and then we had slug soup (it was very good, but I did not know it was slug soup until afterwards); then we had hard-boiled eggs in mince, followed by rice with raisins in it; after that jam dumplings; then we had boiled pork, pieces of mutton and other dishes. *Chang,* which is Tibetan beer, was turned on *ad lib.* I am certain that should I eat such a meal today I would have violent indigestion. But then I was fit beyond words.

Pede Dzong looked entirely different from when I saw it before, at the end of summer. Now it was well into winter; the ground was covered with snow, and yak could be seen digging into the snow to get at the grass. The lake looked even more turquoise. It was truly a sight to linger long in the memory, and I can picture it now just as I saw it then. In the summer it was surrounded by wild flowers of many colours, but now it was surrounded by a blanket of white. The fish were still swimming around and could be seen plainly, for the water is salty and does not freeze.

It was bitterly cold at Pede Dzong, and I was glad to continue our journey the next day. But when the sun was up, from 10 a.m. to 3 p.m., it was very hot. Before and after that time there was a distinct below-zero temperature, yet it was very pleasant when it was not snowing or blowing a hurricane.

The route was now new to me, for when I was with my friend we came down the Rang Chu, and now we were crossing the Nangartse Pass. It was snowing and very cold, and we made but little headway because of the high wind. When we got to a place called Hongo we were invited to have accommodation with the headman there. The heater he had was a big round stove in the middle of the room, and round it we all sat at night and slept almost in the same position.

Next day we crossed another pass called the Karo Pass, 15,000 feet up. From the top we could see away in the distance red-roofed houses dotted here and there in the snow, with the river winding in and out down the valley. On both sides of us mountains rose up to

20,000 feet, covered with the eternal snows.

Geshi Rimpoche said he hoped we would reach Gobsi that evening, and then we could make Gyantse the following evening and rest for a day in the Monastery there. I was glad to hear this because we were making very good time, especially as it was winter and as some parts of the route were most difficult. I said I would be glad of a day's rest without travelling.

"Yes, my son," he said, "you know now why I could not let you travel by yourself across the roof of the world in winter time."

"Yes," I commented, "when I have completed this journey I think I shall be able to tackle any part of the world, but I am enjoying every minute of it and would not have it otherwise. I have perfect faith when I am with you."

"Yes, my son," he replied, "but you must put your faith in God and not in man."

We did make Gyantse the next night and were made welcome again by the Abbot. This time I was with Geshi Rimpoche; on the last occasion I had been with my friend. I was given the same quarters as before and felt quite at home.

We rested there the next day. I slept till about 10.00 a.m. and felt very fit for the remainder of the journey to Ok Valley. The route now was easy. Many trains of yaks and donkeys were coming and going, and the track was well worn. During the day it was very slushy but, when the sun went down, there was a hard frost. So we tried each day to get to our destination before sunset. Travelling in winter in Tibet is no picnic. Five more days it took us to reach Ok Valley. It was the end of my journey, at least for a while, for I was to remain there a few weeks with Geshi Rimpoche and my other friends would be arriving before I left. I was looking forward to seeing them again and having another wonderful meeting.

The Abbot was delighted to see us. He welcomed me now with great joy and told me how he missed me.

Geshi Rimpoche said: "I told you so. What do you do to people you meet when they are so eager to see you again?" and he laughed heartily. I could see that he was having a joke with me about Norbu.

"Yes," I said, "I will always remember Norbu." "And she will remember you, my son."

I was very happy there. Day after day Geshi Rimpoche would give me more instruction and the Abbot himself had come a long way since I saw him last. The talks my friend had given him had a transforming effect. (See *Beyond the Himalayas,* Chapter VII.)

Sometimes Geshi Rimpoche would ask the Abbot to come along with us, and listen also, and I was pleased that the Abbot did so; it made him feel that he was one of us.

It was I who generally set the ball rolling by asking a question. Then Geshi Rimpoche would open out. We were sitting together, the three of us, after our evening meal, when I asked the question: "What can you do with a rigid mind?"

He replied: "I think we covered that ground before, but as you have asked the question I will answer it for you," and Geshi Rimpoche went on: "It is the rigid mind with fixed ideas that shows up its ignorance. This is the type of mind that cannot understand, because a fixed mind cannot receive or give, because it is caught up in its own conditioning, and being caught up in its own conditioning it can only reflect that conditioning which is not Truth. A rigid mind is ignorant, because it cannot see beyond its own ideas, its own beliefs.

"When you begin to understand this you can quickly recognise a mind that is filled with the ideas of others; that is why it is incapable of thinking for itself. You have only to look at intellectuals to see how they are stuffed with the ideas of others, and it is difficult for them to do any original thinking. They may be well read, but what of it? They are conditioned by it, and are merely expressing that conditioning."

"Yes," I said, "I can see why the intellectuals can never do any original thinking, because their minds are filled with what others say, and they are always quoting authorities."

"Yes, my son, that is true. Without pliability there can be no understanding. When one is freed from fixations, it is easy to detect the mind that is rigid, and there can be no truth in a mind that is rigid. Truth is always unfolding the mind that is aware of its own conditioning. Truth is the moving power in the Universe and must also be the same in man, for there can be no separation in Life that is animating the Universe and is active in mankind.

"As man frees himself from his conditioned thought, Life unfolds man's Divine Nature---the Christ that is Eternal and Ever-Present, knowing neither death nor sickness, for It does not live in opposites. This is 'Being' now. But when there is a becoming there is the struggle between opposites---life-death, health-sickness, success-failure and so on. When this struggle ceases, then Reality comes into being *now,* for It is Ever-Present."

"Yes," I said, "I can see that only when the Consciousness is freed from conditioned thought is there the awareness of Being, Being now. I can also see that 'Being' can never be realised through 'becoming', which is always in the future. It is always tomorrow and tomorrow never comes. This is struggle that must cease before 'Being' is realised. It is only when I am freed from the past and the future, freed from conditioned thought, through understanding what

165

conditioned thought is, and how it comes about, that 'Being' is."

"That is true, my son, but, as you are aware of Being now, you still see an outside world. You can be aware of the physical body, also of your mental creations and when you close your eyes you may hear all the sounds of Life---that is the known. That is the relative; it is not Reality. Only when you know that it is relative can you realise that which is beyond, which is not relative---the Unknown. Being now is when you understand that all you see and hear and touch is not creative: then there is an awareness that is Unknowable. It is now! And is not the created but is Creative!

"You see, there is a vast difference between one that is aware of Being and one that is merely becoming. This is the stage that most so-called Truth students are in, they are always becoming. The one that is becoming is caught up in time, but the one that is aware of Being is no longer caught up in Time, for he knows that time can never reveal the Timeless. Tomorrow can never reveal the Ever-Present now. Only in freedom from yesterday and tomorrow is the Ever-Present revealed. Even in the fleeting glimpse one gets when the mind is silent and free from time, in that moment the Ever-Present is realised.

"The Yoga practice is one of concentration on the inner senses when you become insensible to the outer world, but this can never reveal the Ever-Present which is beyond mind."

"I can see that," I said, "I have already experienced the fact that concentration, which is mental activity, can never reveal that which is not a mental activity, which is beyond mind. I have experienced a sense of freedom when the mind has been quietened through concentration; I have also experienced when Consciousness permeates all phases of mind and conditioned thought which is Sumhadi. But this is still becoming, it is the known, and is still not awareness of 'Being'. The known can never reveal the Unknown, the created can never reveal the Uncreated, which is alone Creative. It is only since I have been shown the falseness of becoming that I have realised the Ever-Present: that the Father and I are one.It is not merely an idea in a conditioned mind but actually Creative now where the self has dissolved into the Ever- Present, like the drop dissolving into the ocean is the ocean now, containing the same constituents, just as Spirit in man is the same as all Spirit, for Spirit is not divided."

"I know," I continued, "that I am using Divine reason and I know that Divine reason can never reveal that which is beyond reason, because even Divine reason is of the mind, and reason must cease before the mind quietens down through knowing that it can never know the Unknown, and therefore ceases to struggle. When struggle ceases the mind is quiet, and in that quietness Reality is, because it always is, being Ever-Present, and comes into Being immediately, not in Time but immediately the mind sees that it can never know."

And I added: "I have watched my mind become still when it ceased fabricating; then Reality was there. When I realised that I could never know what Reality was, I knew what Reality was, and my struggle ceased."

"I can see," said the Abbot, who had not even moved, so deeply was he listening to our discussion, "what transformation means; as I have been listening to you, transformation has been taking place; I could see my mind and how it was working and what was hindering the operation of Reality. I could see myself clearly and the falseness of my beliefs, my ideas. I cannot explain the feeling of freedom I have gained; all I know is that I am changed. I am no longer caught up in my old thoughts and beliefs, and truly it is a great burden that has fallen from me."

Geshi Rimpoche was pleased, for he said: "My son, when you

have made such an impression on the Abbot I know that you can make an impression on those who will listen to you."

After a short silence he continued: "Yes, my son, pure thought is not conditioned by past or future, health or sickness, success or failure, good or evil, God and the devil, for these are the product of the mind; these ideas are the result of your conditioning, caught up in opposites. The Christ is free from all this conditioning. The Christ is the Son of God who is not conditioned in any way. The Life of the Father is in the Son and this is now, my son, now at this very moment. You do not have to wait for this to happen because it is always Present.

"There is an active Intelligence in the body and in all bodies. This intelligence is forever active in the *now;* It is beyond the body, although in the body. Yet you do not know what It is, but you know that It is, don't you?"

"Yes," I exclaimed, "by It my food is digested, by It my heart pumps the blood to every part of the body, carrying all the elements necessary to replenish the cells and to eliminate the waste matter; the body is maintained at an even temperature in winter and summer by this intelligent internal adjustment. Yet the created will always remain relative to the Uncreated- Creative. The body like every other instrument will wear out but that which is real---the Consciousness, Life itself---will remain Eternal and Ever-Present."

And I went on to say: "There is no machine created to match the human body, and there is no power outside the body doing all those amazing things, and so I must admit that this is done from within. The most intricate machine created by man is created from within man himself, and therefore we realise that the created can never match its Creator. While the created is in a continual flux the Uncreated remains stable. While the created is relative, the Creative remains Eternal and Ever-Present. Thus we are in constant touch with the Source of inspiration, genius, the limitless Source of Love, Wisdom and Power, for the Father and I are one."

And I felt constrained to add: "When we speak of this we make it relative because it is merely an ideal in the mind, but, when my mind ceases to formulate, then I can experience this Inspiration and genius; I can experience Love and Wisdom, although I cannot define It."

"Yes, my son," Geshi Rimpoche replied, "you will readily see that if you are caught up in ideas, images, beliefs, traditions, you are bound by them and there is no longer any freedom, because you will think and act in accordance with your beliefs, your ideas, your traditions, your limitations, which hinder the operation of Reality, which is greater than all else.

"I can understand now," I replied, "that we create the prison in which we live. If we merely change our ideas, our beliefs, we only substitute one prison for another. I know that some change from one religion to another only because they find orthodoxy restricting, and so they take on some new cult but it is still of the mind, still a prison, the idea of Reality is not Reality. The new prison may be a little more comfortable but all the same it is a prison in which there is still limitation, in which there is no understanding. It is only when there is an understanding of what the mind is made up of that there is freedom from the prison of our own making."

"Yes," said Geshi Rimpoche in his usual manner, "most people are not aware of 'Being'. The proof lies in the multitudes that float on the sea of ignorance tossed by every whim, idea or emotion and are drowned in the effects. The rush here and there to find health and happiness; some even change their environment in an effort to free themselves. But in the effort to demonstrate health and wealth, they flounder in their own conditioning, which is increased through their struggle in the wrong direction. In their confusion they reach to those who claim that they can teach them, yet all these people do is to put them on a rudderless boat and leave them still subject to the storms and waves on the sea of ignorance because they have not the key that opens the door to freedom."

"Yes," I replied, "I have myself listened to people speak of their God as separate from themselves. Their God is a relative God who can do nothing for them because their God is merely an idea of some Being afar off, separate and distinct from themselves."

"I agree with you, my son, that they are caught up in opposites, such as God and the Devil, good and evil, health and ill-health, success and failure, having and not having, sin, suffering and death; these are real to them. That is the error. They are always becoming and therefore never Become. But in 'Being' there is neither sense of error, nor error of sense. Therefore there is no destructive element because in Being there are no opposites, nothing to overcome, nothing to conquer, therefore no fear, no doubt, no good, no evil; these exist only in the mind, and if you look you will see them there. In the mind of man, they flourish because man feeds them by his belief in them; therefore he is conditioned by them.

"Now, if Truth and error co-mingle they produce health and sickness, good and evil, life and death. Then who can say whether Truth or error is the greater" Only through the discernment of the false does the error fall away, because it has no existence except in the conditioned mind. Truth is beyond mind and is free; Truth comes into being immediately we discern the false and understand it. You understand that, don't you?" said Geshi Rimpoche, looking at the Abbot.

"Yes, perfectly," replied the Abbot.

Then Geshi Rimpoche continued: "The power to see and hear does not originate in matter. It must originate in mind otherwise there would be no cognition of what we see and hear. So when the mind is conditioned, the body is conditioned as well. Yet there are those who will say that the mind has no say in the matter, and that the body talks back only when it reproduces what the mind feels.

"We call the body matter, but my Science has proved that the body is energy in formation and the directing power behind this formation is Life. The ignorant makes all things start from the lowest instead of from the highest. Suppose we reverse the process and see the formation from the Source of all things, then in tracing all things we constantly arrive at Infinite Being, where there can be no separation, no error, no opposites, and the physical consciousness in which the error---the illusion ---exists dissolves away and the Consciousness of Reality takes its place immediately. The body has no life apart from the One Life that is Eternal and Ever-Present, so if you cling to the body you lose sight of the Real Life, which is free even while in the body. 'I am the Life'. He who sees me sees the Father, *I am the Lord thy God now and forever.*"

As I watched Geshi Rimpoche I could see his face enveloped in light, and as he stood up and stretched forth his arms in the all-hailing sign I felt as I were being charged with a thousand volts of electricity.

With these last words he finished his lesson to us:

"O Infinite One, Thou didst water the yielding crops that grow without man's aid. All that man did was to plant the seed, and Thou didst mould the earth and sprinkle it with sun and rain.

"I shall not disagree with any man who has not found the way to Thee, for everyone must find the way himself unaided.

"Now I am content that all is mine because I am Thine, O Infinite One."

* * * * * * * *

We sat there transformed, uplifted. My mind was still. I did not wish to think or move. I wanted only to remain in that state of ecstasy which I felt at that moment.

Words cannot explain the full beauty of his wisdom and love, and the words I have written are only fragments of what he said. Yet the ecstasy I can feel, as I am writing now.

After some time he rose and went outside. The sun was beginning to set and we followed him on to the balcony overlooking the valley. Chomolhari stood out like a glittering white giant statue against the orange-coloured background of the sky. As the sun was setting, the colours changed to a mixture of glorious pinks and reds.

The valley itself shrouded in the gathering clouds that covered the snow blanket enveloping the whole valley. Then the colours became darker, moulding into dark blue and purple, and the clouds began to cover the majestic Chomolhari until only the peak showed above them. The sun disappeared behind the Monastery and stars began to show themselves far above, throwing a subdued light over the clouds below.

We watched the whole change with the enraptured thoughts which we had gleaned from Geshi Rimpoche's talk, and the enchantment of this magnificent scene in Nature transported me to another world. Yes, I had the feeling I was not on the earth at that moment.

CHAPTER XV

TIME at Ok Valley was passing unnoticed. Every day Geshi Rimpoche was schooling me for my work in the world I came from and my stay at Ok Valley was coming to an end. This in a way made me feel sad, because of the harmony and love that was always present and which was unknown to me in the world I knew.

Seven days before I left, all our old friends came. There were Geshi Dar Tsang from Yangtang Monastery, Geshi Malapa from Gonsaka Monastery, and Geshi Tung La; Tsang Tapa of Ok Monastery, who was in Lhasa for several weeks, also returned; and my friend came all the way from Zamsar by himself to be with me and to accompany me as far as Kalimpong to the place where he had met me.

It is hard to say whom I liked best. All had their different ways, yet all showed Love and affection. I think I would place them in this way: Geshi Rimpoche, my friend, Tung La, and the others much the same. The Hermit of Ling-Shi-La was not here, though I knew I should meet him again soon.

When my friend handed me a letter I knew at once from whom it was. It was from Norbu. I read it and showed it to my friend because between us there were no secrets. I said to him: "Tell her I will return to Kalimpong in three years from today and I will meet her there and you also."

"Yes, my son, we will meet you there." (And this happened exactly three years to the day. None of us had aged or altered in any way, and that was the most astonishing revelation; it was as if we had never parted.)

What a happy family we were, the eight of us. Geshi Rimpoche, my friend, Tung La, Tsang Tapa, Dar Tsang, Malapa, the Abbot and myself. We laughed together, we talked about many things. Old times were reviewed with greater interest than ever before.

I was keen to know all about what each one had done. It was extremely interesting and pleasing, when I found that I would read Tung La's thoughts and that he could read mine as easily as we did before, even better. The Abbot no longer hung back but took part in the conversation. I could see that he had shed most of his orthodoxy.

Talk about a transformation! I spoke to the Abbot about it.

"Yes," he said, "I have had many long discussions with Geshi Rimpoche since you left and I could see the falseness of my mental repetitions, fabrications and beliefs, so they fell away, and the freedom that I felt was more than words can tell."

"Yes," I commented, "I saw the difference immediately I met you again."

"But the transformation," he explained, "has taken place only since you came. That is the strange thing about it all. Geshi Rimpoche did not speak to me about these things before; it was you (turning to my friend) who stung me out of my stupidity. I can remember very clearly the dressing down I got from you." (This you can read in Chapter VIII of *Beyond the Himalayas*.)

Geshi Rimpoche went to the heart of things but was very quiet in his explanations. My friend was the very opposite. He went straight to the heart of the false and showed it up in its true colours, just that it was false. Geshi Rimpoche was softer, showing you in a quiet way where you were wrong, but my friend struck at the very root and destroyed it. Both were great adepts, yet I could distinguish the great difference in their ways of instruction, and I knew I needed them both.

Again the Hermit of Ling-Shi-La was different, I would not say he was a greater Master than my friend or Geshi Rimpoche, but there was something about him that gave you the impression, "I am not of this world".

Each and every one had his respective place in my life, and I could fit them in perfectly. Tung La, Dar Tsang, Malapa and Tsang Tapa and the Abbot all had their special places in my training, and when I look back I can see it all so clearly. I can see that it fitted into a plan not devised by man's mind but a plan that reaches far beyond the bounds of the mind of man. When we look deep enough we can see that our being on earth at all reaches the understanding of man, beyond the will of man, for we are born of the Spirit of God. "Call no man your father on earth for one is your Father who is in heaven."

One evening in the Abbot's rooms we were all looking out on to Chomohari. The moon was shining on it; the sky was clear, and there were no clouds in the valley; the embers of the great log fire were low and gave a deep reddish glow to the room. The eight of us were present, and all at once the Hermit of Ling-Shi-La appeared in the midst of us. I was not surprised because I was thinking deeply about him just then.

There must have been sufficient ectoplasm in the room for him to show himself, though we were not sitting for that purpose. Then he spoke and I shall always remember the words he said:

"I have come as I said I would, and though I have been with you for some time this evening it is only now that I am able to show myself and speak to you."

I knew what he meant, though he had been with us probably all the evening; my thinking of him was no doubt the sensing of his presence, and there had not been sufficient ectoplasm to enable him to show himself until we began to look on Chomolhari with the same thought.

Chapter XV

That night was a memorable one, especially as no arrangements had been made for a sitting. It was quite a natural and unexpected visit, and this was the best possible way to appear.

Then the Hermit spoke to me and said: "My son, I have come to speak to you before you leave us for that world which to you seems so far away at present."

He spoke in a slow, deliberate manner, as he always did, with the assurance that what he was saying was the Truth and we all knew that it was the Truth.

"We are the expression of Life," he said, "the expression of the Living Presence which is not an idea and which is not dependent on any outside agency. It is the same Living Presence that is responsible for all Creation. If you will note the fact that you are living, then in this living you can see that what you have created in your mind is very far removed from that which is created by the Living Presence. You will note that that which is in your mind is merely what you have heard, learned, experienced or believed. You will see now that these memories will dissolve away, but the Living Presence, that which is alive and is your Livingness, is the Eternal Creativeness and is the only Reality.

"So you see clearly that the Intelligence which built the body existed before It created the body and will exist after the body is dissolved into the substance out of which it has been created. The Intelligence and Substance out of which, and in which, forms are built remain Eternal, for there is nothing outside the Eternal, all is within the Eternal, yet the greatest idea you may ever form in your mind of the Eternal is not the Eternal.

"As I am speaking to you I can see how you are forming ideas as I reason with you. That is good so far as it goes but it does no go far enough. You are still functioning in the mind, creating ideas of what

I say. But if you listen in the deeper sense there is a revealing process that is not made up of ideas. That is what I want you to do, so that you will see what an idea is, because if you are not aware of what an idea is, and how it is formulated, you will never experience that which is beyond ideas. Yet you depend on others and by doing so you perpetuate the illusion of your dependence on others---which is useless. Then you hide behind this illusion and repeat the words 'God is Love, God is Wisdom, God is Life', and such-like words. But there are merely ideas, are they not? You have not realised this before, because you were dependent upon what another said. God can never be a Reality to you when you merely accept what another says or when you depend upon an outside authority, no matter how learned that authority may be.

"In the past you have depended upon what others have said, you have allowed others to influence your thinking, and to some extent you have allowed tradition, beliefs, nationalities, to rule your life, you being unaware of the fact that these things are the cause of separation, fear, limitation, confusion and sorrow."

(Now I could see the Hermit very plainly. Everyone was of course interested in what he was saying, though he was speaking directly to me, and because of their interest the ectoplasm became denser. It was as if I were transported to the Hermitage of Ling-Shi-La at that moment.)

"Now," he continued, "what is the remedy? The remedy is that you must do your own thinking; free from tradition, free from beliefs, free from limitation, free from separation. This is the only way to know the Truth about anything. For if you are caught up in your beliefs, your ideas, you can never know the Truth. You must discern the cause that keeps you in bondage. If you are not free yourself you cannot free another; you must discern the illusion clearly, otherwise there is no freedom. Freedom is *now* , but the illusion of dependence keeps you in bondage. What is in your mind is the old; you must meet the new, free from the old, and this can be done only by knowing what the old is; then you do not meet the new with the old.

"The Livingness that Jesus knew, and what I know, and I hope that you also will know completely, is not something in the future nor in the past, but is Ever-Present, *now*. If you will look into your mind you will see that the future is merely an idea, and when you see the Truth of this it falls away, does it not? You feel free because you know the Truth about it. Your Livingness in the future is merely an idea in the mind, and will ever be an idea of your Livingness yet never your Livingness itself. When you see that your idea of Reality is not Reality you become aware of your Livingness now, because you are not making It an idea. Do you follow me?"

"Oh yes," I said, "I do very clearly now."

"When you see that it is not your family or your nationality or your church or your belief of your traditions that keep your heart beating, you will see beyond these limitations; you will know that it is something that is Ever-Present within, and is not an idea, that is doing this wonderful thing, nor anything external to yourself. Then why do you depend upon an outside source at any time?

"It is written that Jesus said: 'He who comes to me and does not put aside his father and his mother and his brother and his sister and his wife and his children, even his own life, he cannot be a disciple to me.' The meaning of this, if you are dependent upon anything or any person, no matter how near or dear they are to you, you are dependent. Thus you will never know the Real, the Ever-Present Livingness, that is behind all and is in all and is greater than all. You can never be a disciple to the Christ of God unless you realise that the Spirit of God is born in every soul that comes into the world. If you depend on an outside source you therefore cannot be a disciple of the Christ of God.

Chapter XV

"You must steadfastly refuse to worship or be dependent upon any external representative of the Christhood whatsoever. You must worship God in Truth and Reality. When you worship the external you become a slave and bound to the illusion of what you worship.

"Awareness of the false can only be when you understand the false, when you know how it came about. This awareness must not be induced from outside, but through your own discernment of the false, otherwise you will be dependent upon an outside authority again.

"You can be stimulated by an external reaction, but all stimulants are similar in effect; whether you have a drink, look at a picture, go to a concert or a religious ceremony or work yourself up over an act of any kind, noble or ignoble, they are the same, merely stimulants. When you understand this, then they fall away. Then that which is greater than all these things comes into being. This is freedom from all illusion. Then you will understand that stimulation, high or low, whether worthy or unworthy, leads to illusion and not to freedom and truth.

"You have already come to understand that organised religion, politics, cults, nationalities, tradition, are fetters which bind one, making one fiendish in one's beliefs; and this causes strife and misery. This wolf in sheep's clothing must be seen stripped of the clothing it puts on to confuse you, and you alone can do what is necessary. It is not what another says that frees you, for that is but another idea, another belief in opposition to the one you discarded, and they are after all much the same. Only by thinking for yourself is there freedom from dependence upon others, dependence upon beliefs, ideas, cults, and the rest.

"It is difficult for some to withdraw from these things, simply because they cannot think for themselves. Their fixed ideas are too strongly embedded in the mind, and so they are caught up in them.

This is their background and they can think only in terms of that background.

"You will see, my son, that these things cause the mind to be warped, narrow and bigoted. So conflict arises, and this further conditions thought-feeling, causing more misery and setting in operation a never-ending chain of cause and effect that can cease only when you see the falseness of it. When you see the falseness of it, it falls away, and immediately there is freedom and Reality, because It is Ever-Present. So it is necessary to be constantly aware of your thought-feeling reaction; then, my son, you will not be caught up in the net of illusion.

"If you rely on others to give you cheer, hope and courage, however noble, you become lost again in separation and dependence. Groups have a beginning and an ending, and are generally in opposition to each other, causing further confusion. To seek that which has no beginning and no ending, the journey lies within yourself. Every other way is a distraction leading to illusion in which there is no freedom, no Truth.

"When you try to solve conflict and sorrow on its own level, this leads to further sorrow, conflict and frustration. But if you journey on, constantly aware of what is happening around you, you will discern that which is preventing the expression of the Ever-Present Reality---Love. *Then your journey will be a revealing process*, an experience that is constantly liberating and creative. In this alone there is freedom and Truth."

"Now, my son," he continued, "to experience this freedom you must not be dependent on any authority or any individual, however learned that authority or individual may me, for dependence of any kind creates uncertainty and fear, thus preventing the experiencing of the Real.

"In your world today, my son, there is little or no creative understanding in high places. What hope there is, is dashed to the ground through lack of self-knowledge. Without self- knowledge we are led into conflict, sorrow, confusion, bloodshed.

"Only through understanding what the self is, can you get beyond the self into that calm, undisturbed, serene state of Being which has the assurance of the Ever-Present Reality--- Love and Wisdom.

"You do not create the Ever-Present Reality, but the Ever-Present Reality becomes operative when the self knows itself to be the hindrance to the Real.

"The self is the cause of the evil, and Jesus realised this when he said, 'Get ye behind me, Satan,' and as you watch you will become aware of the Inner, the Inner that is Love, which is the Intelligent expression of Reality; and as the Inner becomes realised the outer becomes clear. Now this is not something that is separate from another but is the Real in you as it is in another, for there is no separation in the Real, there is no division in Reality.

"Then the evil will be seen as the expression of man's mind in confusion, and it has no existence whatsoever except in the self, which is the illusion, being a bundle of memories and ideas in conflict.

"When you understand this, my son, you will be able to see the outer with its cunning deceits, its deceptions, its unrealness in which so many are lost. Ignorant of the cause of this confusion and misery they accept public opinion which rules them through thought-feeling- reaction. Now you understand what I mean by a revealing process, my son.

"It is common to hear those people rebel against the conditions they themselves unknowingly create, because they never give a thought to the cause and effect which arises from their own thought-feeling-reactions. Surely then it is most important to discern your thought-feeling-reaction and to understand it. Then only can there be freedom from it.

"You will note, my son, that if one follows a certain belief then one will accept anything that will confirm that belief. But if something arises contrary to that belief it will be rejected without question. *So they squirm and wriggle without thinking, so their ignorance remains.*

"There is no distinction, no separation, when you realise the immediate Presence of Reality. All are alike, the first and the last and the last and the first are all the same, for they are one in the Living Presence.

"There cannot be separation and therefore there can be no distinction; all is one in the Kingdom of the Ever-Present Love. The last to realise it is just the same as the first. We are all in Infinity now, for we cannot be outside it, as there is no existence outside Infinity, but most people do not realise this because they are caught up in separation and distinction.

"Now, my son, when all understand this, we will all live joyfully in the Cosmic Temple of the Living God, to the glory of the Father and the Brotherhood of all mankind."

The he lifted his arms in the all-haling sign of the Master and said:

"O Blessed One, in our ignorance we sought Thee in the outer, but could not find Thee. "It was only when we saw the outer was unreal did we seek deep in our Being to find the pearl of great price.

"The beliefs in which we thought we could find inspiration, we found was chaff scattered before the winds of fear and doubt.

Chapter XV

"It was when we spread Thy wings of Love beyond the boundaries of separation that Thou didst leap into our hearts with joy

"Then we knew Thee as the Christ within Thy only begotten Son, O Blessed One, O Blessed One."

* * * * * * * *

There was a deep silence for some time after the Hermit had spoken. Then he turned to

Geshi Rimpoche and said: "I will return when you have your regular meeting in three days' time. Then our son will leave for the world he came from and we will watch over him until his work is completed."

Then he left us. I watched his magnificent figure dissolve away in the midst, and I felt I wanted to go with the wisest man in all Asia.

CHAPTER XVI

It was a beautiful winter's morning, the air was crisp, and the sun rising from behind Chomolhari was a sight for the gods. The morning seemed brighter, the sunrise seemed more magnificent, and Chomolhari more beautiful. The sun's rays were spreading over the sky from behind the mountain, showing up the peak like a giant diamond in a setting of sparkling colours, with a background of twinkling stars which had not yet receded into the cloudless blue sky.

As I stood on the balcony watching this panorama of colour changing into brighter and brighter hues, gradually lighting up the whole blue canopy overhead, I heard the Lamas chanting *"Om Mani Padme Hum"*.

I was in a sort of dream. I was thinking of the Hermit of Ling-Shi-La and the wonderful experience of listening to him again, when I felt someone beside me. It was my friend; he, too, had come to enjoy the magnificent scene before us. He put his arm around my shoulders in his usual affectionate manner and said:

"I knew you would be here this morning, my son. I saw you deep in thought, silhouetted against the white snows of Chomolhari and surrounded by the rays of the rising sun. It was the most inspiring picture I have yet seen. You stood in the centre as the rays spread wider and wider around you, your head and shoulders seemed magnified as you stood out against the white snow-covered mountain, the peak reflecting the rays of light to all the world. I was startled by the magnificence of it all. My thoughts were about you and your work to come, and though I shall not be with you in the flesh, my son, I shall be with you in spirit."

"I want to speak to you this morning about action, so let us sit down," he said; and we went over to a seat that faced the rising sun and sat down together.

185

He did not begin at once but sat in silence for a while.

I could not measure the actual time, for time had disappeared. But during this period I felt as if a silent transformation were taking place within me, and in the midst of the silence I could hear his voice. I seemed to be listening deep within me to what he was saying.

"The individual is what the world is, and without transformation of the individual there can be no transformation in the world, for the individual is the root of the strife in which the world now lives.

"Now, my son, people believe that collective regeneration must come before the individual is free from confusion and conflict. But the reverse is the case, for without individual regeneration there can be no freedom for the masses; because, without understanding the relationship of the individual, there can be no regeneration, for the individual is not separate from the whole."

I could listen to that tone of voice for ever--that was how I felt at the moment.

"We are the product of the whole," he continued, "though each one may be conditioned socially, religiously, racially or politically according to his environment. You will see that, though each one may be conditioned differently, the total process of separation is this conditioning. It is only when you understand this, that there is radical transformation; because you see how you have become conditioned.

"Now, my son, the world is crying out for action of some kind; we all want to act. We want to know what to do especially when the world is divided by ideologies which oppose each other and with so-called religious groups putting man against man.

The world is in such confusion, such misery, such chaos, but we do not realise that this is because of our own behaviour, for we are the world.

"Now, action by itself is non-existent. Action can be in relation only to a person, to a thing, to an idea. So the first thing we have to do is to understand action, and in understanding this we shall be able to act rightly.

"Action is merely behaviour, is it not? So if we act in accordance with our conditioning we are merely conforming to a pattern, and that is merely reaction, not action, and because we do not know how we have acquired this pattern we are caught up in its net.

"If we try to fit our action into an idea it is no longer right action; it is merely conforming to a pattern, is it not? I want you to watch carefully, so that you can understand this vital question, as you will have to face it in the world to which you are going back.

"Therefore, to understand action, you must understand the false process of conforming to a pattern. This aggressive action of conformity cannot be right action, in which there is no reaction; conforming to a pattern is the cause of confusion and strife, because you do not understand the falseness of it. Therefore your action is the continuity of a pattern in opposition to another pattern, and this can never bring peace and harmony. But if you know the false as the false, the false will fall away and you will have the True.

"Right action is your peaceful approach to Life Itself, not the aggressive approach to Life, trying to make Life an instrument for the fulfilment of your own desires. This is merely an expression of the self which inevitably brings sorrow and conflict. This action is the result of an idea and is not the true action which only operates in its unlimited state when you are free from the false.Only when you understand the false can you act rightly, and through relationship can this be best understood. You understand that, my son?"

"Yes," I replied, "it is obvious that there must be a complete transformation in our relationship with each other in every walk of life, because things cannot go on as they are. This is self-evident to anyone who is alert, watching the individual and collective activity in the process of conforming to ideas, to traditions, to systems, to patterns whether they be religious, political or social, which is leading us to the brink of disaster and which is staring us in the face. To ignore it or become complacent about it does not stem the impending avalanche. Only by understanding the cause can there be right action that leads to regeneration."

"I can see," I continued, "that there must be action that transforms now, and not in time, for time can never reveal that which is Timeless, and only in that Timeless state is there tranquillity, freedom, peace and happiness."

"Yes, my son," he answered, "that is what we are concerned with. Everywhere throughout the world there is strife, poverty, dirt, communal struggle, strikes, minor wars. These eventually develop into a global struggle, which never solves the problem because the false is not understood.

"To discuss this intellectually is of no avail; there must be an experiencing of what is said, within, otherwise there can be no transformation. You must forget what another has said, and I am not quoting anyone; that would be stupid, for you cannot understand by quoting another. You can understand only when you are not following another. You must find out for yourself; otherwise, you will be merely conforming to what another believes.

"If you follow an idea there can be no understanding, you are merely conforming; so it is important to find out which comes first, the idea or action. If the idea comes first, then you are conforming to the idea and this is merely imitation according to the idea, and this means antagonism. The whole structure of our civilisation is built upon opposing ideas; that is why we have confusion and conflict. Is not the world divided over opposing ideas? Without understanding the whole process of ideas, and merely to take sides, is stupid and infantile. It is the sign of the immature. The mature person tries to solve the problem of human suffering, war and starvation, but to take sides is to be conditioned one way or the other; then there can be no solution to the problem.

"If ideas shape your action, then by that action you will only create more misery and confusion. But when you see that your action is not based upon an idea, upon memory, then there will come a state of affairs that never needs to be overthrown and rebuilt as is taking place everywhere today.

"You will see that this state does not conform to an idea, and that is possible only when you understand what an idea is, how it is brought about, and how it moulds your action.

"Action that is moulded from an idea is detrimental to true action. To look for the solution through such action is to look in vain. Only action that is not based upon an idea can bring about a regeneration that is ever-renewing, free from struggle and free from the antagonism of conflicting ideas. Do you understand, my son?"

"Yes," I replied.

"Then you can see," he went on, "that a power or scheme that dominates is utterly evil and stupid. To force others to think what ones them to think brings eventual disaster to oneself and others. This has been shown again and again throughout history. You create the schemer, the leader, because you are confused; and because of your condition you turn and rend your leader and schemer.

"The only power is the power of Love, of understanding, of kindliness and mercy; this power of Reality alone is liberating.

Chapter XVI

"A mind that is caught up in schemes, in power, can never know love, and without Love there is no solution to the problem. You may postpone understanding, you may intellectually avoid it, you can build these bridges which are still temporary, but without goodwill there is bound to be ever-increasing misery and destruction. This is evident to the man of sense. What we need in the world today is not more ideas, not more blue prints, not bigger and better leaders, *but goodwill, affection, Love and kindliness.*

"Therefore what is needed is people who love, people who are kind and that must be yourself, myself, not somebody else; because if I am not that myself, I cannot expect anyone else to be. If you are not loving and kind yourself, how can you expect another to be loving and kind?

"Love is not worship of a God, for are you not all worshipping some kind of God whom you have made up in your minds, which has become a belief in opposition to another worshipping a different God, creating another belief?

"Some worship an image, a statue of stone or wood, or some conception of the deity, and this is a marvellous escape from one's own brutality or the brutality of another, but it does not solve the difficulty. *Love is the only solution.* To Love your neighbour as yourself---and your neighbour is everyone you meet. That is Truth, my son. . It must not be merely an idea but an active transformation within; for what the inner is, so the outer shall be. That is the Yoga of the Christ."

He had just finished when Geshi Rimpoche and the Abbot came out and sat down beside us. Shortly afterwards the others followed. The sun had risen by this time, and it was getting quite warm as it always does when the sun is up.

This balcony was Geshi Rimpoche's favourite spot in the

morning sun, and it was where he generally had his morning tea. Soon afterwards several Lamas came out with the usual Tibetan tea, which I had come to enjoy just as much as the others did.

There was a general conversation and when Tung La edged in beside me I felt he had something to say, for I could read his mind. He started speaking in Tibetan and I replied in English for practice. Then Geshi Rimpoche came over to us in a happy mood saying: "You two mind-reading again?"

I replied with reverence: "It was you who started it, you know."

At this we all laughed, for our mind-reading had become quite a joke by now, and in the evening we often made a game of it, and seldom were Tung La or I wrong.

We were all very human, knowing as we did that there was no such thing as a superhuman being; that was merely an idea and not the truth.

Everything was natural, it is only those who are caught up in their own stupid conceit who make things unnatural, and that is ignorance personified.

It was a lovely morning and we remained on the balcony enjoying the sun. When lunch-time came Geshi Rimpoche said: "Come, my son, and have some lunch," for I always sat at his right hand.

When we were all seated at the table we were in the same positions as we occupied when we had our seance. These places were always kept afterwards, when we were all together---my friend at the other end of the table, Dar Tsang on his right, Malapa on his left; the Abbot on Geshi Rimpoche's left; Tung La on my right, and

Tsang Tapa on the Abbot's left. (If you refer to page 159[1] of *Beyond the Himalayas* you will see the plan.)

There was never a dull moment. We were alert, our minds always clear and sensitive. It was a joy to live in this atmosphere. After meals Geshi Rimpoche gave thanks for what we had received.

After lunch, he announced that we would soon have our next meeting and there meet our friends again as we did before---those who had left the body, and some who were still in the body like the Hermit of Ling-Shi-La. This would take place, he said, on Sunday night in three days' time, as had been arranged between himself and the Hermit of Ling-Shi-La.

I was overjoyed to hear of this, because several times I had been on the verge of asking Geshi Rimpoche when we were to have our next meeting, because my time was getting short. I had now only six days left and I wanted to make the most of this precious time with all my friends, especially with Geshi Rimpoche; indeed it was for this purpose that he came as far as Tragste Gompa beyond Lhasa to wait for me till I returned with my friend from Zamsar.

After lunch Geshi Rimpoche guided me to his private quarters. Every afternoon he would do the same, for it was the time he liked best to talk to me. I felt that this day he had something very important to speak to me about.

He commenced by saying: "My son, time is drawing near for you to leave us. In one way I feel sad and yet in another way I am glad. I am sad because you will not see me again in the flesh, though I am glad that I shall be with you always in spirit, for the time has come for me to leave this earthly body I am now using."

---

[1] **NB: [In the original publication only]** - page 89 in reformatted version.

Chapter XVI

I felt sad when he said this, but I also felt glad when I knew that there was no death, no separation in or out of the body, and I said so. His face always lit up when I mentioned this. I had become very attached to him and he knew it.

"Now, my son," he said, "remember your problems can never be solved by following another, for this prevents the understanding of yourself. It is very easy to follow someone; the greater the personality, the easier it is to follow. Yet this prevents Creativeness, because the follower can never be creative. It is when you understand this that you become original, no longer a gramophone putting on the records. I am speaking to you directly, this being the best means of transformation; you understand that, don't you?"

I nodded, and he went on: "When you are face to face with yourself in your relationship to others you will know what you are, for relationship is the mirror in which you see yourself. But this is often unpleasant, and you do not want to look at yourself; so you try to escape by following someone, and thus you live in the shadow of another while you condemn and criticise. Some turn to the latest phase of new thought as a means of escape, merely to avoid seeing themselves.

"To see oneself there must be no condemnation, no acceptance, no justification, no identification. If you are aware in this way impersonally, you can see what is taking place in the superficial, and your deep hidden reactions become screened before you. This can be done only when you understand the process of thinking.

"Your thinking arises from memory which you have accumulated, and this is your conditioning. It is when you understand this, that there is awareness of the self and its ways; for the thinker is not separate from his thoughts. When you see this you do not try to separate yourself from your thoughts; you begin to understand them, and when you understand your thoughts you understand yourself, your conditioning.

"Why do you want to isolate a thought and look at it? Why do you want to hold one thought and try to escape from all other thoughts? If you look into your mind you will see why! You think by dwelling upon one thought and suppressing others you can free yourself from them. But this is impossible because you will find that the suppressed thoughts rise up to distract you from the one you have chosen. Now you can see that you can never understand yourself or your thoughts in this way, and without knowing yourself there can be no right thinking.

"You have in the past called this meditation---to choose a thought and isolate, by concentrating upon it, thinking by doing so that you are meditating. But this kind of meditation can never free you from the burden of your conditioned thinking.

"Why do you choose a particular thought upon which to dwell? It is because you think that by doing so it will give a reward or pleasure, so that you can hide behind it. But this very desire to dwell on it creates a resistance against all thoughts which pour in. So you keep up a constant battle between the thought you have chosen and all those which you try to suppress.

"You can see clearly now, I hope, that you cannot understand your mind in this way, neither can this give you the freedom you are looking for. But when you look at each thought as it arises and uncover its meaning you will see that these thoughts never come up again. They are finished with. It is only the unfinished thoughts, the thought that is not understood that rises again and again.

"So the important thing is not controlling your thoughts but understanding your thought. If your mind is narrowed down, limited, controlled, shaped according to its own desires and the influence of its environment, its accumulations, obviously it can never be free. This process of isolating yourself for self-protection brings exactly the reverse, for in doing so you must engender fear, and how can a mind that is fearful ever be open to that which is Real in which there is no fear?

"When you see that *you are your thoughts* you will begin to understand. But if you imagine you are separate from your thoughts you look at them as separate from yourself and then fear them. But when you know they are your own creations, those creations no longer influence you. In this understanding, only, is there freedom, and in this freedom there is the Real. *Then you will see that there is no conflict between the thinker and his thought. And the mind is no longer agitated.*

"When this is understood the mind becomes quiet; it is not made quiet. A mind that is made quiet or disciplined can never know the Real; it is incapable of receiving the Real.

"You can discern a mind that is so conditioned. It is bound, it is petty, and God is made petty by a petty mind. It is when thought-process comes to an end and is no longer fighting and struggling with opposites that the mind becomes free and still. In that stillness there are wider and deeper states of Being. But if you merely pursue the deeper it becomes imagination, speculation, and this must cease before the *Real is.*

"Therefore understanding is the beginning of meditation, and true meditation is the gateway to Reality. There are no tricks to learn, no technique to follow, for that would lead you away from the first principle of freedom and self-knowledge, and without self-knowledge there is no freedom.

"You must see things as they are, then you understand yourself. Only in this way is there stillness of mind and in this stillness Reality operates in Its unlimited state of Being.

"In this way, my son, is there true inspiration and that is what we want. A free mind, free from the accumulation of the past, freed from all that is hindering the Real, the New. You must meet the new without the hindrance of the past, the old."

I had heard similar words before, but now they had a deeper significance; they had a deeper transforming effect. There was an understanding and a freedom that I knew could not be had by any form of concentration of the mind on a single idea or thought. I felt as if all the past were rising before me and I knew it was the self which had no power except the power I gave it. My fears were my own illusions created by my own conditioning. When I saw this I felt that freedom which does not come by any other means except through understanding myself.

CHAPTER XVII

THE evening arrived which was arranged for our meeting. The sky was clear, not a cloud in the moonlight canopy overhead, filled with twinkling stars all shining like diamonds. The moon was full and seemed to be in the same position as when we had our last meeting. But now everything was white, the valley and Chomolhari being completely covered with snow. That beautiful mountain stood out like a white guardian reflecting its beauty and silhouetted in the moonlight against a background of millions of diamond-like stars twinkling in the moonlight blue sky giving the appearance of veiled daylight.

The whole scene was one of exquisite beauty and, though it was freezing outside, there was a warmth about us that was not created by any artificial means, for everyone in the room was an adept in Tumo and sufficient heat was created without our even practising it.

There was a happy harmonious anticipation, and the atmosphere was electric.

I felt that this night would be a great success; conditions could not be more perfect. Geshi Rimpoche spoke to us in the way he had done before at our last meeting (described in my book *Beyond the Himalayas*).

He said: "Love is not the word 'love', the word is not the thing itself. God is not the word 'God'. But most people are satisfied with the word because of the response that the word creates, producing certain nervous reactions because one has fed on words.

"But words are empty; they merely produce a nervous response. This is not Love, neither is it God. It is only when you know what a word is, and how it forms ideas in the mind, that you will understand that God is not a word, neither is Love a word.

"Words only create reaction. That is why everyone know reaction, but few know action, because action can only come when you understand that the word 'Love' is not Love and the word 'God' is not God.

"We can know what Love is only when we are sensitive to the feelings and sufferings of others. But most people do not want to understand suffering; they want to escape from it, through prayer, through a Saviour, through ideas, through concentration, or reincarnation, through drink or any kind of addiction, or any means whereby they can escape.

"When you are hungry you do not discuss how to eat, you want food and you are not concerned how you get it. So you can understand suffering only when you know your own thoughtlessness, your stupidity, your narrowness and brutality. Then when you look at suffering you will not want to escape from it but to understand it. In this way you become keen, watchful, alert to the cause of suffering, and then you are not callous, you are kind not merely to those near you but to everyone.

"When you understand suffering you are sensitive to the suffering of others. There is no escape, and because there is no escape there is kindliness, there is affection.

"Affection-Love demands the highest intelligence and without being sensitive there can be no great Intelligence. Only the intelligent know that the word 'Love' is not Love and that the word 'God' is not God. In understanding this, then Love is, God is."

I knew what he said was true, I felt it within me. There was a deep transformation and we remained in this silence for several minutes, and, as I knew that the word "God" was not God, "I knew", but I could not tell what it was that I knew. I think we all felt the same.

Then he spoke again: "Conditions are even more perfect than we had our last meeting, and we shall have many more friends with us tonight!"

It was what he said that created these excellent conditions. I could see the whole room being filled with clouds of ectoplasm forming into one big cloud. I felt as I did before, even more so, that I was up in the clouds above the earth altogether.

The outlines of the forms were becoming quite clear, when I heard Malarepa greet us with his usual blessing as soon as the seance was in full swing.

Then Malarepa spoke to us all, not to anyone in particular. He said: "I listened to our brother, Geshi Rimpoche, and I hope you gained the understanding that was implied.

"God-Truth-Love is not something that is apart from you, for God-Love is Eternal and Ever-present and is the only Reality. But God Love cannot be realised by a mind that is confused, conditioned, limited. How can such a mind realise Reality-God which is unlimited, unconditioned? The mind first conditioned itself, therefore it must free itself from its own limitations, and then only can it realise that which is beyond it, beyond limitation, beyond ideas, beyond words.

"Reality is the Unknown and words can never reveal the Unknown.

"The self invents Reality because it imitates, it copies, it has read so many books each having so many ideas, and it merely repeats all these ideas and experiences of others, words, words, words. If you look into your mind you will become aware of what a word is, and then you will no longer copy or imitate, neither will you repeat what another says because the Truth is greater and is beyond words and ideas. These, you will see, are the creations of the mind, but Reality is not created.

"Most people prefer to read religious books and to speculate about God, rather than seeing what they are themselves. But without understanding the self, what the self is, there can be no realisation of the Real."

Then he came over to me and said: "Your work will be a joy to us, my son; we will follow you and help you and protect you. Your work is to expose the false. You must be ruthless with the false; you must show it up in all its falseness, for that alone can dissolve it. Refuse to be caught up in a net of words in regard to it, for there is no case for the false, for it is false and that is the Truth about it. Neither must you minimise it or cloak it in any form of Reality, for that would be a lie. No matter how the false has embedded itself in the minds and hearts of the people, even if it may be their most cherished beliefs, you must in no way agree with them because of their inherited belief, but reveal the falseness of these mental creations, for they are not the Real.

"The Real is all-inclusive and not exclusive. Anything that separates man from man is false and that is what ideas and words do. So the Truth cannot be found in words or ideas, written or spoken, and only when you realise this is it possible for the Real to operate, and in that operation there is Love and unlimited Intelligence.

Then Malarepa went over to speak to Tsang Tapa, the oracle of Ok, the medium he used to speak to Geshi Rimpoche, and supply him with food, when Geshi Rimpoche was snowbound in the Himalayas. (This I have related in my book *Beyond the Himalayas.*)

In the meantime the Hermit of Ling-Shi-La came to me and I was delighted to see him again within a week; it reminded me of my visit to him. He appeared to me just as he was; that was the wonderful thing about it. His face was lit up as if the sun were shining through it. I had grown to love the Hermit and he knew it, for he showered me with affectionate thoughts and blessings. I knew now, that I had wonderful friends.

He said: "I have followed you every step of the way. I was with you on the mountain Nyiblung Richung of the Nyenchentanga range, the range of mountains that you see from the Hermitage. You know you were only about forty miles as the eagle flies from Ling-Shi-La when you were at Zamsar, but there is no track over the mountains, it being unexplored country, and so you had to take the roundabout way, 150 miles to reach Zamsar."

Then he continued: "I am very pleased with you, my son, you found much to think about at Zamsar."

"Yes," I said, "I did. We went into much detail and I had great enlightenment."

"No," he went on, "I want you to realise that, out of chaos, order cannot come. You cannot create order by bringing about chaos to do so. This is the false thinking of many of the people. Many think that they are chosen by God to create confusion and disorder in order to bring about order. But this only creates further disorder. This is the cause of constant repetition of wars and economic disasters.

"You look for transformation in the future so that ultimately these conditions will be no more. But it is always in the future. Now, a mind that is always thinking in terms of the future is not capable of acting in the present.

"Do you understand the true meaning of transformation, my son?"

"Yes, I do, I know that transformation in the future is impossible. It can only be now, moment to moment --- when we see the false as the false and the true as the true, when we see the false in that which has been accepted as the true, as we see that *now* there is transformation, now.

It does not happen tomorrow, it must be now, otherwise there is no transformation. So when I see the false I also see the truth about the false, that it is false, and it falls away; now, immediately, there is transformation and in transformation there is liberation."

"Yes, my son," he said, "when you see that repetitions are the projection of a mind that is bound, when you see the truth of this then there is transformation. When you see what creates separation, conflict and misery, there is immediate transformation and the very truth of it is liberating. The very perception of Truth is transforming and liberating, and it is immediate, not tomorrow, for there must be transformation now; otherwise there cannot be transformation.

"You will be surrounded by the false in the world to which you are returning.

"But the very perceiving of the false, moment to moment is transformation. You cannot find Truth through memory, through time, for Truth is 'now', not in the past of in the future. You cannot find Truth tomorrow, nor in what you read or hear, for that is merely ideas. Truth comes to you, you do not go to Truth. When you are going to Truth it is merely a projection of yourself. It is when the self is understood that Truth comes and It is immediate. Eternity is Now! The now is NEW, and not a reflection of the past, for that is memory; neither is *NOW* the future, the future is of the mind. *The Now! is alive.* The past is dead and the future is not yet born.

"You cannot discover the new if you approach it with the old. Only when you know that you cannot experience the new while burdened with the old does the old cease to project itself into the new. You see, my son, it is from moment to moment; even the moment that is past cannot be ever-present now. What is in the mind is a hindrance to the new; therefore you must approach the new fresh and not conditioned by the past; only then can you discover that which is renewing moment to moment.

"When you desire to be transformed there is no transformation, because you are thinking in terms of becoming. Truth is 'Being' now moment to moment. Truth cannot be found in a book, It can only be found moment to moment, in the smile, in the tear, in the embrace, in the fullness of Love. Without Love Truth is not. Where there is Love there is transformation, because Love is 'Being' moment to moment. That is Truth, my son.

"When you leave here we will be with you, for there is no separation in the Spirit that lives in each one. God is not divided. It is the conditioned mind that hides this great Truth. In knowing this, my son, your faith will be constant, and your Love will be liberating, never binding. For a love that binds is not true. Love that binds is of the mind and Truth-Love is beyond mind and is the only Real."

Then he stood aside and said: "Now your august spiritual guide, St. Anthony, will speak to you."

I was anxious to speak to St. Anthony, for I had spoken to him so many times all over the world, and had felt his influence so often in my work.

His words were differently expressed from the others, though the same Truth was revealed. He put forth his hand and said:

"Touch my hand, my friend; now you see I am functioning on your plane by means of the magnetic substance which is a phase of the Substance out of which everything is created. There is only one Substance underlying all forms, all manifestations, though there are different degrees of that Substance and you have all these degrees of Substance now with you. You are functioning in and through them all, though you are not aware of them. At present you are functioning in what you call the material, but that is merely a modification of the one Substance; it is a degree and not separate.

"As you leave the physical or material you will still function in the same Substance but of a different degree, and this will go on through the various degrees which become finer and finer.

"In your work you will be using what is known as the magnetic body, that is the body that can be charged with vital energy suitable for the physical; you will also use your mental and spiritual at the same time. I do not mean the psychological side of your mind but a substance which interpenetrates both your astral and magnetic sheaths.

"The Spirit uses all these sheaths accordingly, and when we are helping you in your work through the centre that is linked into these sheaths, according to the conditions of the patient.

"When you feel inspired to speak of the Spiritual things of Life we are working through the finer sheaths or centres. But Truth is above all these; Truth is Life-Love. Love comes into Being when the mind is freed from the past---the old. Love is always new, and you can meet the new only when the past---the old---is understood, when it falls away.

Therefore to meet the new you do not meet it with the old or it will be merely the projection of the old. But when you see that the old is memory, experience, and that it can never be new, then you know, and when you know you meet the new knowing that the old can never be the new. The new is always new and never old.

"That is Truth, that is Love, because it is Real. Therefore the new is the only Real, the old is not Real, it is memories, experiences, which often condition you.

"True Spiritual Healing is when you are free from the old, for Spiritual healing is always new. Do you understand me?"

"Yes, I do," I replied. "I can see that Spirit is always present, always new and never old. Spirit is always renewing. The renewing of the Spirit is moment to moment, in which there is no disease, no death, no past, no future. There is only the 'Now' and the 'Now' is always new. In this I have true inspiration, that is not the result of the past, or memory."

"Yes, my friend," he said, "I see that you understand, and with this understanding your work will be of greater value to the world, and you will be of great value to us who are working with you for the transformation of the world.

"You will not merely be repeating what you have read. Most teachers in the world today are gramophones putting on the various records. But you must be the musician and the music. Only in this way are you creative."

Then he said: "There are others here who want to speak to you."

This meeting was the greatest I have ever experienced. Many friends came who had passed on. Two Yogi friends, Abdul and Seelum, brought me some apports, some tablets of ancient Egypt and some precious stones and golden coins of Tiberius, in all about twenty articles. One was an ancient vellum written in ancient Greek; in the left hand bottom corner was a deed of sale in Roman cursive. It had apparently been sold at one time, probably in the first century. (I received a similar one at Mr.Bailey's seance in Sydney some years afterward.)

One of the ancient Persian Magi spoke, and naturally my mother and other friends. The meeting went on till about 3 a.m., six hours of constant contact with those who had passed and some who were still on the earth plane; sometimes there were ten or more in the room at the same time.

There is no greater proof of survival than this direct contact; all fear of death passes away with the understanding of Life Everlasting. Many intimate things were spoken of, and news of people at home and other information was accurately given. This I found to be true on my return.

The advice that a friend had passed from the earth life on a certain date was given. Some would hardly believe it possible, yet it is a fact, for I verified it when I returned home.

At the end a brilliant light appeared and in that light the Master appeared and blessed us all. This was the crowning point of the whole meeting, the knowledge of the Eternal Living Christ Who exists in all hearts, in all realms.

"In my Father's house are many mansions, and I go to prepare a place for you and where I am there shall you be also," these were the words he spoke clearly and distinctly.

This closed the meeting.

We sat in silence for some time, each with his own thoughts.

Soon now I would be leaving my wonderful friends from whom I had gained so much, This passed through my mind and I felt a little sad. Geshi Rimpoche must have sensed it, for he put his hand on my shoulder (I was sitting next to him) and said: "My son, I feel as you feel. I am aware of your thoughts but there is no real parting, as has been proved to you tonight. Therefore rejoice in the understanding that God alone lives and we are living and moving in Him and He is living and moving in us. So there can be no separation except in the mind and that is an illusion, *as you know*."

We sat talking for more than an hour, when I felt extremely hungry and said to the Abbot: "You know, I feel I would like something to eat. I don't know why."

"Well," remarked the Abbot, "we are just about to have breakfast. It has been prepared."

The Abbot had apparently arranged everything beforehand, and breakfast was brought in by two of his personal attendant Lamas. It was more like a dinner than a breakfast. Geshi Rimpoche broke bread and blessed it and spoke in very endearing terms about my coming, my stay and my going. I felt deeply humble as this great sage spoke for in his heart there was a Love that was beyond human comprehension.

Here in this room were my beloved friends, friends who were more than friends, sages who were Masters of Nature, whose knowledge, Love and Wisdom are unknown in our world of conflict. Yet these great adepts are helping those in our world who will open their hearts to God through understanding the conditioned state of their minds, which is the only hindrance to the healing Power and Love of Reality.

The sun's rays were beginning to show up from behind the peak of Chomolhari and we went out on to the balcony and watched the gigantic splendour. This morning it seemed even more wonderful, as the sun rose; the rays of colours spread upwards like a giant fan with the peak of Chomolhari in the centre. The white crystal-like snow reflected this dazzling splendour while the Lamas chanted "*Om Mani Padme Hum*", their deep voices becoming louder and louder. The impression of this scene is vivid in my memory as I write now.

When the morning chanting was over we rose and went to our respective quarters. I went to bed and slept. I do not know whether it was a dream or not but I was consciously mingling with those who were not of the earth.

I must have slept till midday, when I felt an influence beside me; when I opened my eyes Geshi Rimpoche was standing looking at me. He said: "You are now refreshed in Spirit, Soul and body."

I replied: "That is just what I feel like."

"When you get up," he said, "we will wander down the valley, for I want to talk to you. You will be leaving us tomorrow and I want to have you to myself today. Although there is no separation in Spirit I feel your going as if I were parting with my only son."

After we had some food we wandered down the valley in the snow towards Chomolhari. I said: "I feel very sad to leave you, and more so when I think that I may not see you in the flesh again, for you have been more than a father to me, and I have grown to look upon you with a very deep affection."

"Yes, my son," he replied, "and my affection for you was long before you saw me in the flesh, for I have been with you a long time in your work. But now I will soon lay down my life to take it up again, freed from the physical. I will no longer come back to it, but will sojourn in the other realms; yet I will still be with you, like your venerable guide, Saint Anthony."

He added: "There is a proverb that says: 'Get wisdom, get understanding, forget it not, neither decline from the words of my mouth.' Yet there is a higher and better way, 'Love your neighbour as yourself.'

"Love is the solution of all problems and God is Love and Love is God. Yet people approach Him with hate in their hearts towards others. The Divine can only be approached when the heart is full of Love and the mind empty of antagonism.

"You see, my son, a person who follows a certain religion and is antagonistic to another who follows another religion becomes irreligious. So the so-called religious man is more dangerous because he is pursuing ideals which divide mankind by putting one against the other.

"You realise, my son, that ideas divide man more than things do. There are also those who have leanings to the left and those who have leanings to the right; they are merely pursuing ideas. The one thinks his idea is better than the ideas of the other, and this leads to antagonism, strife and bloodshed. Peace and Love can only come when it is seen how ideas and beliefs set man against man.

"Only when man gives up the illusion of the importance of his ideas will Love come into the heart and mind of man, and this will be immediate, immediately man see the false. Man will then appear in the likeness of his Father who is Love, having a natural dominion over all things, which is not being supernatural, as many believe.

"Jesus never claimed to be supernatural, yet people have built up in their minds an idea of the supernatural and then worship this, their own mental illusion. By worshipping, they try to escape from seeing themselves as they really are with all their antagonisms, hate and jealousy. Only by seeing the false can the true come into being now. That is wisdom, my son. Only by understanding the false and how it comes about does wisdom come into being. Thus only is there freedom from the bondage in which many struggle.

"When wisdom comes you will realise that not a blade of grass, nor a flower, nor a tree, nor a bud blooms, of its own volition; you will realise that there is nothing on earth or beyond that has not its source in the Infinite One.

"Therefore, you will no longer be mute before ignorance, nor dumb before the false but you will correct the error through understanding. You will no longer ask what the trouble is but you will show the way to the solution of all problems.

"The highest form of thought-feeling comes through understanding and not through the aggressive self-assertiveness of ideas and beliefs. We can only find the source of our Creativeness in Reality, in Love. Therefore you will no longer seek security, for he who seeks security is ever in want. The very basis of your security is in knowing and not seeking. For you live now in the ever-present, never-ending Source of Supply."

I listened most carefully. I had gained the art of listening without creating ideas, but by understanding the self, for self-knowledge was freedom and transformation, and in this Freedom Reality operated without limitation or any kind.

I was no longer the same person as when we met first. My psychological philosophising had disappeared, for I knew now that it did not matter very much whether it was true or not, in fact it was mostly a hindrance to the Real, being merely mental gymnastics.

This was the final talk that Geshi Rimpoche gave me. It was a sort of final advice, though he never sought to give advice. It was mostly a cleansing through understanding, which could be done only by oneself alone.

Then he said: "I will not return to Lingmatang with you as I had intended; I will remain here for the winter, and as I look upon that beautiful mountain as the sun rises and sets I shall be thinking of you, for it is here I love most of all. But your friend will accompany you as far as Kalimpong, and then you will be on your own physically, but not spiritually.

"Here is a cross, a symbol I have had since I was a boy; it was given to me by my father. You will notice there is a diamond set in the centre where the perpendicular and horizontal bars meet; this represents the Son, the conformation of the Father-Mother-God. The son is born in Love and Wisdom, which is Truth.

"I want you to keep it on your person always," he said gently.

He then took it from around his neck and put it round mine, and then he blessed me. Tears ran down my cheeks and I did nothing to check them, for I felt as if the Christ had awakened in my soul at that moment. From then on I was never the same, it was as if I had put off the beggar's robe and put on the Robe of Love---the Yoga of the Christ---and even though the hem alone be touched it would heal the troubled soul.

CHAPTER XVIII

I was up before sunrise, as my friend and I were to leave after breakfast on our journey back over the Himalayas on our way to Kalimpong.

The feeling I had that morning was similar to that which I had when a boy leaving the Highlands of Scotland, where I always went for my holidays, and on returning to school there was a deep feeling of sorrow, for I loved the hills and the heather, the lochs and the rivers. It was much the same feeling I had that morning, and I said so to my friend.

Everyone was up for breakfast. The Abbot was waiting for me. He put a silk scarf around my neck as a parting gift. It was so fine that I could put it in a small envelope. This gift is traditional and significant to the Tibetans, and it means a great deal to the receiver; coming from the Abbot it signified an eternal blessing.

On the following day all the others, with the exception of Geshi Rimpoche, the Abbot, and Tsang Tapa, would be leaving Ok Valley. Tung La, Malapa, and Dar Tsang would be on their way back to the valley of Ha Chu.

Dar Tsang would be going to Yantang Monastery, Malapa to Gonsaka Monastery, and Tung La to Takohu. Such a gathering of adepts would not take place again for many years.

We all sat down to breakfast together in our usual places.

Then Geshi Rimpoche stood up and said: "Once in a lifetime on earth for each one of us there is a memorable occasion; that is why we always remember such an occasion, because it stands out like a great mountain peak above all other peaks.

"You will all agree with me that such an occasion has just come to pass in our lifetime in this isolated land of ours on the roof of the world.

"My beloved son here has been with us now for nearly seven months and now he is about to depart from our midst. We may not see him again in the physical but we will in the spiritual, for we will be helping him in his work which is our work in his world. We have all come together twice in a short space of time, and now all of you will again go back to your respective places, but with greater understanding gained from his presence amongst us.

"He will be leaving an indelible impression upon us and there is no need to tell you who he is, for we all know that he was with us in the ages past and now has returned with the soul- experience necessary for his work in this time. We also know that we shall meet again, and with this knowledge the parting is made much easier, so we bid him adieu for a while. He carries with him our love and blessings and the Love of God will remain with him always."

Then he made the all-hailing sign that is familiar to all adepts, and sat down.

I was conscious of a power surrounding me as all eyes were turned towards me. I rose and said: "All the words I could say would not reveal what is in my heart," for I had found real Love, a Love that speaks more than words and which alone could solve all problems. The problems affecting mankind were created by man himself and could only be solved through the heart and not the mind.

"I have come to understand," I said, "what the mind is made up of and how it is conditioned. When I look into our relationship like a mirror I see the fact very clearly without prejudice and that very perception brings about a transformation without effort.

"When I see the fact as it is, then that very fact is the Truth which

214

resolves the problem. When I see that the self is the problem, when I see this fact, without endeavouring to escape or hide from the truth of it, then there is transformation which alone can bring about a solution of the problem.

"When I recognise the truth of this fact then there is a quietness of the mind in which conflict ceases. In the quietness Reality-Love is, and when Reality-Love operates there is no problem, for the self will have dissolved away. It is very simple and the simple person can understand, for understanding is not for the few but for all.

"Reality is *now*! Therefore transformation is immediate. Time does not reveal that which is Timeless. Therefore when I see what is now, and become aware moment to moment, without the past-memory, the old, hiding the new, then the new is renewed moment to moment when I meet the moment free from the past and this is possible now.

"I can see," I said, "what my message is. It is not merely giving more ideas to already burdened minds but to show how false and binding ideas are, for ideas of the mind can never reveal the Truth, can never solve any problem. Only Love can, and Love is immediate when the conditioning of the past, of beliefs, of memories, is understood and dissolved.

"I am more than grateful for the love and wisdom I have gained by being with you all and I leave you with a heavy heart. You know I would like to stay with you, but that is not possible because I must fulfil the task allotted to me, and I am joyful in the knowledge that you will be helping me in this task."

Then I blessed them all with the all-hailing sign, for I was now privileged to do so, having passed all the tests given me to perform.

After breakfast my friend and I left while the rest stood and watched us from the balcony.

As we departed at sunrise, the Lamas were chanting *"Om Mani Padme Hum"*. It was as if the whole Monastery were bidding me farewell.

The sunrise that morning was particularly beautiful, and Chomolhari, the lovely mountain which I had looked upon so often at night and in the morning, seemed to know the love I had for it, as it reflected the rays of the rising sun, like a sparkling jewel.

We turned our faces towards Phari. We crossed a number of streams which now were frozen over. We saw two snow leopards, which stood looking at us. The plains were utterly bleak, nothing to be seen for miles except wild yak and hares. The cold wind swept down from Chomolhari over the plains towards Phari. In summer this plain is a mass of colour, with wild flowers in profusion. What a difference today, covered as it was with a blanket of snow.

We met several trains of yak and donkeys as we entered Phari, the highest and coldest and filthiest place in all the world. Innumerable beggars sat in the cold snow spinning their prayer wheels and holding out their hands for alms. The women now had their faces smeared with a combination of yak blood and earth to protect their skins from the frost, wind and sun. The combination of these three makes the skin very sore.

The streets were choked with garbage built up through the centuries, and urchins ran about in their bare feet unaffected by the cold, impervious to the dung and filth. Dead dogs lay in the streets, no one even bothering to remove them, while the dogs that were alive fed on their companions' carcasses, apparently the only food they could find.

We reached the Phari bungalow about 4 p.m. Plenty of wood

was there, so we lit a big fire and had a good meal. I was glad to get away from Phari and I said so to my friend. Yet the people there seemed happy under such dreadful conditions.

Next morning, after breakfast of fried eggs on toast, we made our way to a place called Gautsa, about sixteen miles away. On looking back we could see Chomolhari glittering in the sun, and in front of us a vast plain with hundreds of yak digging in the snow to get food. Foxes and hares in their dozens were there, everything looking for something to eat.

We met a train of yak carrying wool, and some donkeys. This is a common sight and pleasant to see. The track here was up on the mountainside, great crags of rock hanging overhead.

We reached Gautsa after crossing a bridge built in two sections, the old and the new. The hut was in a tiny village of wooden houses. In one of the sheds there were a number of muleteers drinking *chang* (Tibetan beer) making merry. Even when intoxicated these Tibetans are a happy and cheery lot of fellows; seldom if ever do they quarrel among themselves.

My friend talked to them in Tibetan, and as we were both dressed in the robes of the Lamas they did everything the could for us. In the big shed these fellows began dancing and singing. Some of the dances were extremely strenuous; they whirl at a terrific speed round and round, and their cloaks almost fly off. They kept up the dancing till the early hours of the morning.

The track in the early morning was quite frozen, but as the sun rose it became slush with the melted snow and mud mixed together.

The track followed along the riverside, the Ama Chu, which flows through a gorge between two mountain ranges over 15,000 feet high. It was a rushing mountain river even in winter, but in summer it would become a violent torrent as the snow melted in the mountain.

As we came to the end of the gorge we could see Lingmatang, where we were to stay for the night. I was glad because we were well known to the Abbot, and it was here that I first met Geshi Rimpoche.

We entered the Chumbi Valley and made our way to the Monastery. Lingmatang is situated at the end of the valley, at the mouth of the gorge. In the distance we could see the town of Yatung, the first Tibetan town of any size over the Himalayas.

Here we saw a number of wild sheep call Burrhal. Wild bears come down from the mountain woods and raid the crops. The nomads here have mastiff dogs to protect their animals from prowling leopards and wolves.

When the Abbot saw us again he was overjoyed, and he prevailed upon us to stay with him for two nights, which we did. We were glad of the rest before climbing the last range of mountains that separated us from the outside world.

The Chumbi Valley even in winter is beautiful. Yatung is a prosperous town of stone houses with shingle roofs, studded here and there along both sides of the Ama Chu.

During my stay I slept in Geshi Rimpoche's quarters, for it was his desire that I should sleep in his quarters while I was there. We fed well and rested well, for we would now have to cross the Jepel pass. The Natala was impassable during winter. We had now reached the range of the Himalayas separating India from Tibet.

We were sitting quietly after our evening meal in Geshi Rimpoche's quarters and I felt his influence. So did my friend, for he gave us a brilliant talk.

He said: "Peace is not the denial of conflict. Merely to deny evil does not make you virtuous. If you deny the ugly, are you beautiful? The pursuit of the opposites is never peaceful, neither is it virtue or beauty, for the opposite is always in conflict. The very denial of anything creates conflict, and virtue can never be the result of denial of the opposite. Peace is not the denial of war, for war is the projection of ourselves.

"Is it not so that the idealist is causing more trouble than one who does not follow an ideal? The fact is that ideals divide man more than things do. I know you have heard similar words from Geshi Rimpoche but I feel I must repeat them, so important is this understanding to your work.

"Is it not a fact that those who have leanings to the right and those who have leanings to the left are merely following ideas? It is because one thinks one's ideas are more important than the ideas of another that leads to conflict, war and hatred. Reconciliation is only possible when we see what ideas are and how they divide us.

"We call ourselves British, American, Russian, Chinese, Indian, and all the rest. We cling to a group because we want to be safe. This identification gives us a sense of security. But the identification with any group means separation, disintegration and war, in which there is not security.

"It is the dream of every ideologist to have every one believing in his ideology whether it be the right or the left. But such a thing is impossible, because believing always separates. Therefore it is a disintegrating factor and not a uniting factor.

"So long as there is conflict inwardly, psychologically, there must be the projection of this conflict. So without understanding our own inward conflict while trying to gain peace, organisation has no meaning.

"Merely to resist war and maintain an inward psychological conflict, creates only further conflict. But if you understand the total process of inward conflict that causes war then you are neither a war-monger nor a pacifist; you are entirely different, because you are at peace within yourself; and therefore you are at peace with the world.

"So it is not that you should belong to this or that, or be one thing of the other; what is necessary is to understand the cause of conflict.

"You change enemies from time to time and you seem to be quite pleased with yourselves, and this is kept going by propaganda, by your inward psychological conflict.

"So you encourage wars through ideals, nationalities, through greed, through aggrandisement. You encourage war inwardly and then outwardly. You want peace, but this is surely the height of stupidity, the ranting of immature minds always in contradiction.

"You want to become something---a war hero, a millionaire, a virtuous person, a pacifist and all the rest. The very desire to become involves conflict.

"There is peace when there is no desire to become, and when you see that becoming is going away from the Real you cease to become, and when you cease to become then there is Reality---Creativeness.

"You will no longer be seeking security, for the mind that is seeking security is ever in fear and can never know the joy of Creative Being. The very basis of your security is in knowing and not in seeking.

"The highest form of thought-feeling is acquired through self-knowledge and Divine comprehension, and not in the aggressive self-assertiveness of the idealist.

"The mind and heart must be peaceful, quiet then you will know what it is to be without conflict.

"As every war produces another war, so each conflict produces another conflict. To end conflicts you must understand the self, for only with self-knowledge is there liberation from conflict inwardly and outwardly.

"When you are grappling with the problem of mass murder, hunger and misery and destruction on your own level, you create further misery. You are only concerned with the reorganisation of greed, ill-will, and there is no end to the confusion and antagonism which will remain until you deal with its roots, and these roots are deeply implanted in yourselves.

"It is now clear---is it not?---that if the reformer has not radically transformed himself by seeing that the problem is his own, there can be no inner realisation of true values and anything that he contributes will only add further conflict and misery.

"It is often through suffering that you are awakened out of your mortal dream to realise that you alone perpetuate your own suffering. Then the less you think of ways and means and the more you begin to understand yourself, the sooner will you have peace that is an Eternal value and not the conflict of opposites.

"In the lips of him that hath understanding wisdom is found: but a rod is for the back of him that is void of understanding."

I was still listening for some time after he had finished. I had now learned how to listen, not to the words but with a deeper understanding where I saw myself, and in doing so that very seeing was liberation and transformation.

I could see that the Abbot also was in deep meditation, a meditation that was self- revealing, for it was true meditation, not merely concentrating on an idea to the exclusion of all else, for there could be no liberation from conflict or realisation of the Real in that way.

That night I slept well and felt rested and refreshed the next morning, and was ready to climb the Jepel pass.

We made an early start and reached the hut half-way up, and there we rested for the night. We had been travelled for eight hours in deep snow, sometimes the snow where it had built up into a drift being up to our thighs.

The next day I thought would be worst, and I was hoping that there would not be a snowstorm, for a storm on the pass is a dreadful experience. The wind is fierce and you cannot see more than a few yards in front of you, this being quite common at this time of the year. The snow piles up into high drifts on the track, making progress almost impossible. I had one experience of this and did not want another.

As it happened we had fair weather all the way. The sun was hot (even in the middle of winter it can be uncomfortably hot).

When we reached the top of the pass we could look down towards Gangtok, the capital of Sikkim.

Just over the pass there was another hut, where we stayed for the night. We made a log fire and had our evening meal. Afterwards we sat by the fire till the embers showed only a red glow, and the candle gave a dim veiled light to the room.

I could feel the influence of Geshi Rimpoche and I was sure that he was present. I said so to my friend. He was conscious, too, of the same influence and said: "Let us be quiet for a few minutes, and he may become visible." We did so, and it was not long before we saw the form of Geshi Rimpoche building up before us. This time I could see him plainly and I was no longer ignorant about these visitations.

I could see his lips moving and could just hear his voice faintly saying: "You see, my son, I am still with you." Then the Hermit of Ling-Shi-La appeared and said: "Have the faith that moves mountains, my son, and we will help you through that faith. Never doubt but act, and in that action Reality will operate. Remember, it is the Spirit of the Father that doeth the work."

Then they both disappeared again, I was overjoyful; my confidence was such that nothing could shake it.

I said to my friend: "This is the most wonderful evening I have ever had. It means more than even than the evenings which were prepared. Those few minutes were to me Eternity Itself."

Needless to say I slept like a child that night, and in the morning I was still affected by what had happened the night before. I could still feel the influence of Geshi Rimpoche and the Hermit of Ling-Shi-La, and the whole meaning became more significant.

On our way down towards Gangtok, the capital of Sikkim, my feet were on wings; I had the lightness of a bird, a heart full of joy. My mind felt as if it were silenced for all time, and that feeling of ecstasy has always remained with me. It has kept me young, as was proved when a friend, who had not seen me for twenty years and had heard that I was in his country, decided that he must see me, thinking of course that I was then an old man. When he saw me his exclamation was: "Good God, you don't look a day older, what is the secret? I said: "I have no secret, I am just what I am." Yet he himself had grown old.

We arrived at Gangtok that evening. I felt sorry I was back in civilisation again. It was a peculiar feeling; I could not say that I disliked it, yet when I thought of the other side of the Himalayas I felt a tinge of sadness. At the same time I felt an eagerness to get down to work, for now I had something to give, whereas before I was not sure. *And that feeling of not being sure made me feel a fraud, for I felt within myself that I did not really know.* But now, I knew the false. Yet before, I thought the same false to be true. Now I knew differently, and I wanted to get down to my work as soon as possible.

We paid our respects to Mr. Gould and had dinner with him that evening. The conversation veered round to what I had done all those months, for my acquaintances had lost track of me altogether. But when I told Mr. Gould what I had done, and where I had been, he could hardly believe it.

For I had been where no other living white man had ever trod--- in the unexplored parts of Tibet. This was only possible by being with the Tibetan adepts.

I found that most people were more interested in where I had been than in the Truth Itself. Yet Truth is the most important thing in Life.

The next day we drove in a small baby Austin to Kalimpong---the end of the trail.

I can, as I write, still experience that feeling of loneliness when I said good-bye to my friend. Tears ran down my cheeks, yet I was not emotional. I felt that I had lost my crutches and could hardly stand by myself. My friend must have read my thought for he said: "It is best that I leave you now, for the Spirit that is within you will support you for the rest of the way. You are not alone, for He, who created you is by your side, and He is greater than all, for He is all. He is Wholeness: He is Life Itself. The Father has Life in Himself and grants the Son to have the same Life in Himself.

"You have learned to be independent, yet you feel dependent. This illusion of dependence keeps you in bondage. If you rely on others to give you aid, hope and courage, however noble they may be, you become lost in dependence and separation.

"If you depend upon that which has a beginning and an ending, then there is fear. But when you see the Truth of this fact you will then find that which has no beginning or ending, and that is within you. Everything else is a distraction, leading to ignorance and illusion. Reality comes when you are freed from the illusion of dependence. If you discern your thought-feeling-reaction now, you will see how false it is: then the false will drop from you. Then you will know that there is no separation between us, because there is but 'One', and in Him there is no division, no separation.

"There is no distinction, no separation, in the immediate Presence. There cannot be separation, therefore no distinction. We are in the Kingdom of the Ever-Present Love, the last to realise it is just the same as the first, for all are in the Kingdom *now*, but do not realise it."

He then put his arm around my shoulders and said: "My son, I am with you even unto the end of the world." Then he turned and left me.

I watched him go. I waited for him to turn but he kept the same steady step that I knew when I first met him. When he passed out of my sight I said to myself: "Is it all a dream?" I stood there for I don't know how long. Then I came out of my dreams and I knew this was no dream. I knew what my task was and I knew I would fulfil it, no matter where it took me, all over the world. And all over the world I went. In every corner of the globe I gave the message of freedom.

At that moment I thought of Norbu, and the promise that I had made to see her and my friend in three years' time came back to mind.

"Yes, "I said to myself, "it is all real." I did not know how this would happen but it did happen, how I could not say. Things just came to pass all dovetailed in such a way as if by some unseen agency.

I have written this book mostly for the purpose of revealing the false, and only by knowing the false can you realise the True. Then the Truth will set you free.

THE YOGA OF THE CHRIST

O Mighty One, I myself am nothing but with Thee I am all
there is, Thou art not divided.

When I reasoned Divinely and observed the false I cleared the
way for Thy Living Presence.

In Thy Living Presence I saw no evil because Thou art the only One;
evil I saw was of my own mind.

I saw there could be no Reality in personality because Thou
alone art Real and Indivisible.

I saw there could be no Reality in sin because in Thee there is no
sin and Thou alone existeth. Only in the mind of man does sin dwell
and the mind of man is false.

Truth is all there is, Truth is indivisible because there is nothing else
to divide It. Truth is unchangeable because there is nothing else to
change It.

When I saw what blinded me to the Truth I died with the false.

Now the Truth has set me free knowing that in myself was the error
believing the false to be true.

Now that the self has died, my Life is Thine, Thy Life is mine, for
evermore, O Blessed Eternal Living Presence

O BLESSED ETERNAL LIVING PRESENCE

Favor

If you enjoyed this book, may I ask a small favor? Please go back to Amazon and leave an honest review of *The Yoga of Christ*. Reviews help us spread the word of Dr. MacDonald-Bayne to the world more effectively, and sustain our efforts. We appreciate your continued support.

Thank you,
Barry J. Peterson

INTERESTING READS:

"Science and Health, 1875 Edition", Mary Baker Glover (Eddy)
www.ScienceAndHealth1875Edition.Com

"The Sickle" by William W. Walker   www.TheSickle.Org

"The Quimby Manuscripts"   www.TheQuimbyManuscripts.Com

Reading to the Dead, a transitional grief therapy for the living
www.ReadingToTheDead.Com
Author: Barry J Peterson

Neville Goddard: The Complete Reader
www.NevilleGoddardReader.Com
Author: Neville Goddard

www.AudioEnlightenment.Com

GNOSTIC AUDIO SELECTION:

To access the streaming audio book version of
"Yoga of the Christ"
please visit www.GnosticAudio.Com and follow the directions
to access your free streaming audio version of this publication.
This is streaming audio only; the audio book is NOT downloadable

Visit www.AudioEnlightenmentPress.Com for the latest publications
from the world of Metaphysics

upp Todd

OPP - THOT

BBUSI - SiJNaL.